The Photographic Guide to
Schooling Your Horse

LESLEY BAYLEY

Photography by Bob Atkins

David & Charles

Contents

Schooling 8   **Flatwork** 47   **Lateral Work** 103

Polework   119   **Jumping**   125   **Western Riding** 141

Useful Contacts   158

Acknowledgements 158

Index 159

Introduction

• Bob Mayhew (top) is a respected Western rider, trainer and judge. He has a Quarter Horse stud in the UK and was one of the first Europeans to become a judge of reining in the USA. His horse is the Quarter Horse stallion, Fast Draw Peppy.

• John Bowen (above) is an international and Olympic trainer accredited with British Dressage and British Eventing. His horses are Rio and Rupert. Rio is a chestnut Dutch warmblood dressage and jumping stallion. He is seven years old. Rupert is also seven and has won Pre-Novice events and Novice dressage competitions.

• Camilla Shepherd (opposite) is an event rider. For the photographs she rode her 10-year-old intermediate event horse Haddon Rising Son.

Many years ago I had my first experience of riding a 'proper' dressage horse. I can still feel his wonderful canter: he felt so powerful and yet was so light in the hand. I had to do so little; he was remarkably easy to ride compared to many other horses. A while later I rode my first flying change – a magic moment when another schoolmaster reacted to my thoughts and a subtle alteration of weight. The two incidents certainly made me look at schooling horses in a new light, and whenever I need to motivate myself I close my eyes and recapture the feelings of those special moments.

However, the very words schooling, flatwork, dressage or training, can have a rather strange effect on some riders! If they have not yet experienced the sheer pleasure of a few moments of complete harmony with a horse they may be reluctant to work on their horse's training. Yet once they start to develop their own and their horse's skills on the flat they reap the benefits elsewhere – for instance in jumping coloured and natural fences and in negotiating gates or other hazards when riding out. A little time devoted to schooling your horse regularly will be a great investment in his future – and in your enjoyment of him.

This book aims to show you that schooling is both enjoyable and essential. A progressive schooling plan will ensure that your horse is a pleasure to ride – he'll be more supple, co-ordinated and in balance, and he'll be interested in his work. Correct schooling is a vital foundation for any horse, whatever discipline he is ultimately aimed at, and is invaluable in allowing him to reach his potential. Hacking, eventing, riding Western or doing show classes – in fact anything you do with your horse – will be helped by educating and training him.

If you care for your horse there's an even more powerful reason to ensure he is schooled regularly and properly: it can prolong his working life. Horses that have been schooled will carry and use themselves more efficiently and, therefore, remain sound longer.

Schooling

Most people want to enjoy riding their horse, whether that pleasure comes from a leisurely hack in the countryside or a 24-hour endurance ride, jumping competitively at a high level or just popping over an occasional fence. Underpinning each rider's enjoyment is their ability to control and direct their horse.

Take the example of the endurance horse that has to travel over undulating terrain at all speeds, negotiating hazards such as river crossings, wooden bridges and narrow paths along the way. The horse needs to be balanced, obedient, responsive, supple and co-ordinated. The rider has to be able to manoeuvre the horse's forehand, move the quarters over, take one step here and so on. All this is possible if the horse is well schooled.

The jumping horse can be asked to shorten or lengthen if he's been trained well on the flat. The show horse can move up several places if the judge finds he's a good ride. The benefits of schooling are enormous for both horse and rider, irrespective of your level of riding or competition.

Schooling Goals

What are we trying to achieve with schooling?

We'd all like a responsive, obedient, forward-going horse who is happy in his work. For this, your horse needs to be supple, calm, relaxed and paying attention, and there's no way he can be if he's uncomfortable, either physically (see Causes of Physical Discomfort, opposite) or mentally.

Mental distress can occur if a horse is overtaxed in his work or if a rider uses aggression or bullying tactics as part of the 'training' programme, and if he is unhappy it will reduce his ability to learn.

By schooling we are aiming to strengthen and supple our horses so they can develop their potential as athletes. This is not an overnight process – the work needs to be systematic and logical so that you can build musculature and improve joint flexibility. Gymnastic exercises, including school movements ranging from changing the rein to shoulder-fore, where the horse's forehand comes off the track a little (see p.108) and the use of poles, are the means to this end. They are used to work on the horse longitudinally – from poll to tail – and laterally – from side to side.

Whenever a horse is handled or ridden he learns something; it's important that the rider realises this and ensures that all lessons are positive ones. A rider must therefore be:

- able to ride in an effective and balanced manner;
- clear in their own mind about what they want to achieve;
- clear with their aids so that the horse knows what is expected;
- consistent in how they ask their horse for a desired response (this means being consistent in how you ride your horse at all times, whether in the arena or on a hack or trail ride);
- quick to reward their horse for the slightest try – positive reinforcement is an effective training aid.

• In order to learn, a horse needs to be comfortable in his body and mind. Look at this horse's tail swinging, indicating that he's relaxed and comfortable.

• Look at body language, eyes and muscles to find out whether your horse is relaxed.

• Strong muscles and flexible joints are produced through plenty of careful schooling work.

CAUSES OF PHYSICAL DISCOMFORT

• Aching muscles because of incorrect work and/or too much of it.

• Muscle tension or spasms.

• Back pain, perhaps due to ill-fitting tack or bad riding.

• A sore mouth caused by incorrect bitting, a dental problem or a heavy handed rider.

• Poor shoeing, which can put a horse out of balance.

• A skeletal problem, such as rotation of the pelvis, that the horse tries to compensate for in his movement, and which thus affects the musculature in other parts of the body.

Key skills to be attained

Let's look at some of the qualities we are looking for in our horses when schooling: relaxation, balance, rhythm, straightness, free forward movement, suppleness, impulsion, engagement.

Relaxation

This horse is relaxed both physically and mentally, he trusts and accepts the rider's aids, he accepts the bit, and he is working forwards in a steady tempo.

Balance

Your horse's balance has to be controlled both longitudinally and laterally. A horse that is drifting sideways is not in balance, neither is one that is running on as he will be moving too fast and will be pulling himself forwards rather than propelling himself from behind. A young horse will have difficulty balancing himself and a rider, and will often change rhythm to compensate. This young stallion shows good balance in his trot work. Correct schooling has enabled him to carry his own weight and that of his rider with ease. He can also easily make changes of direction and speed. As his training progresses, he will learn to shift his centre of gravity towards his quarters, lightening his forehand and working in a more collected frame (see Collection, p.14). When a horse can carry himself easily and efficiently while remaining in balance through all movements, he has achieved self-carriage.

Collection

As his training progresses the shape or frame a horse makes when ridden will alter. Horses naturally carry more weight on the forehand – the distribution is about 60 per cent forehand and 40 per cent hindquarters. One of the purposes of schooling is to gradually build the muscles and the horse's ability to carry himself. As the hindquarters become stronger, so the horse will be able to take more weight behind, so altering the weight distribution; ultimately he will be able to lower his croup and lighten his forehand. This collected frame enables him to move with spring and elevation in his steps, which makes him feel very powerful but very light to the rider.

In collection the horse's frame is shortened, but this should not be achieved by pulling in his front and restricting him. True spring and elevation comes from the powerful hindquarters. Achieving collection is a gradual process.

Rhythm

This is the regularity of the steps or strides within each gait. Each of the steps or strides should be even, covering an equal distance and being of the same duration. There should be a clear beat in each pace, for example a walk beat is 1,2,3,4, while a trot beat is 1,2, 1,2. Tune in to rhythm by saying the appropriate words to yourself when riding. If your horse has a rhythm problem that isn't caused by discomfort (see Get the Beat, below), try slowing everything down, which will make it easier for him to balance himself and keep his steps regular.

GET THE BEAT

If your horse's rhythm is erratic it might be because:

• he's young and finding it difficult to maintain a rhythm all the time. Give young horses regular, short, schooling sessions to improve strength, fitness and rhythm. You can help him develop rhythm by maintaining an even rhythm yourself. For example, in rising trot repeat the beat to yourself as you ride – 1,2 1,2. Working over trotting poles will also help, as will unridden lunge work, including over poles.

• he's evading you – for example, he's not going forwards properly. Your horse must learn to go forward immediately from the lightest of aids – you should only have to tell him to walk once and he should stay in walk until you give him another instruction. If he doesn't respond to leg aids don't simply kick harder. Instead, reinforce the aid with your whip, applied just behind the position of your leg. Be prepared for your horse to shoot forward – you don't want to catch him in the mouth and confuse him. Be clear and consistent in your application of the aids. Constant nagging with your legs will deaden your horse to the aids and make him less pleasant to ride.

• he isn't using himself as well as he should, possibly due to a muscular problem – have him checked by a specialist.

• he isn't level, in which case you should seek veterinary advice.

Straightness

For a horse to be a truly strong athlete he must use both sides of his body equally well. Just as humans have to work at being ambidextrous, so do horses, as, like us, they are born one-sided. Most horses favour their left side and it is the rider's job to correct any crookedness, otherwise the uneven weight and pressure on the limbs could lead to him breaking down.

Even when a horse is ridden on a circle (above) he must be straight, his hind feet following in the tracks of his fore feet. The alignment of his spine also needs to be considered – the spine should correspond to the line he is travelling on, whether that's curved or straight.

● Only the two forelegs are visible in this front view, his shoulders are directly in front of his hindquarters.

● A common fault is for the quarters to be slightly to the inside as shown here, because the rider has lost control of the outside shoulder. See shoulder-fore for correction.

Contact

This is the connection between the rider's hands and the horse's mouth. Whether the contact is firm or light will depend upon the horse's stage of training: lightness of contact comes when a horse is in self-carriage. Think of your arms as being an extension of the reins, ie they belong to the horse. As he moves your contact needs to be elastic so that you maintain a consistent feel, following his movement. Check that your hands are level – it's a common fault for a rider to be stronger on one side and to therefore take a stronger hold on that rein. In addition be aware that he is accepting the contact evenly on each rein and seeking it from you, rather than you trying to establish the contact by pulling on the reins.

• To be straight, a horse needs to take the contact evenly in both reins and move both hindlegs evenly. In the hindlegs, evenness is revealed in stride length and stride height. If you can feel your horse pulling on one rein more than the other, he is not taking an even contact. In the bottom picture the rider is asking the horse to work too deep in order to encourage the horse to be more relaxed over his topline.

Free forward movement

Your horse must go forwards off a light leg aid, moving freely with plenty of activity and relaxed muscles. He should stay in the gait you have asked for without you having to remind him constantly with your leg aids.

Suppleness (right)

When the horse is using his body efficiently with elastic muscles and engaged joints, he is supple. A supple horse can carry himself much better and travel over the ground with less wear and tear on his joints than a stiff, unbalanced horse.

Impulsion

This is the propelling force that results in the horse springing forwards off the ground. It is not speed but is a controlled energy, stemming from an increased activity and mobility in the joints in the horse's hindquarters. Transitions help to build the carrying capacity and the power of the hindquarters.

Engagement (right)

A horse has to be supple before he can engage his hindquarters and this engagement is something that builds over time. When a horse is engaged, the hindquarters carry the majority of the weight, allowing the forehand to become light – his withers will be higher than his haunches and his shoulders will be free, allowing him to really lift and extend his forelegs. You can see here the flexion of the hock and how much the horse's hindleg is coming underneath his body.

23

What stage have you reached?

Before you can embark on any schooling programme you need to know at what point you are starting. If your horse is young and green you have a very clear starting point – you are right at the beginning and your first priority is to get your horse going forwards and straight. If he has had some schooling you need to assess how successful or otherwise this has been.

As your horse's training progresses, and his balance and self-carriage improve, so will his ability to respond to your requests to ride deeper into the corners of the arena.

● An advanced horse demonstrating how a novice horse would work into a corner. The novice horse does not have sufficient balance and weight-carrying capacity in his hindquarters to allow him to go too deeply into a corner. Compare this with the photograph opposite.

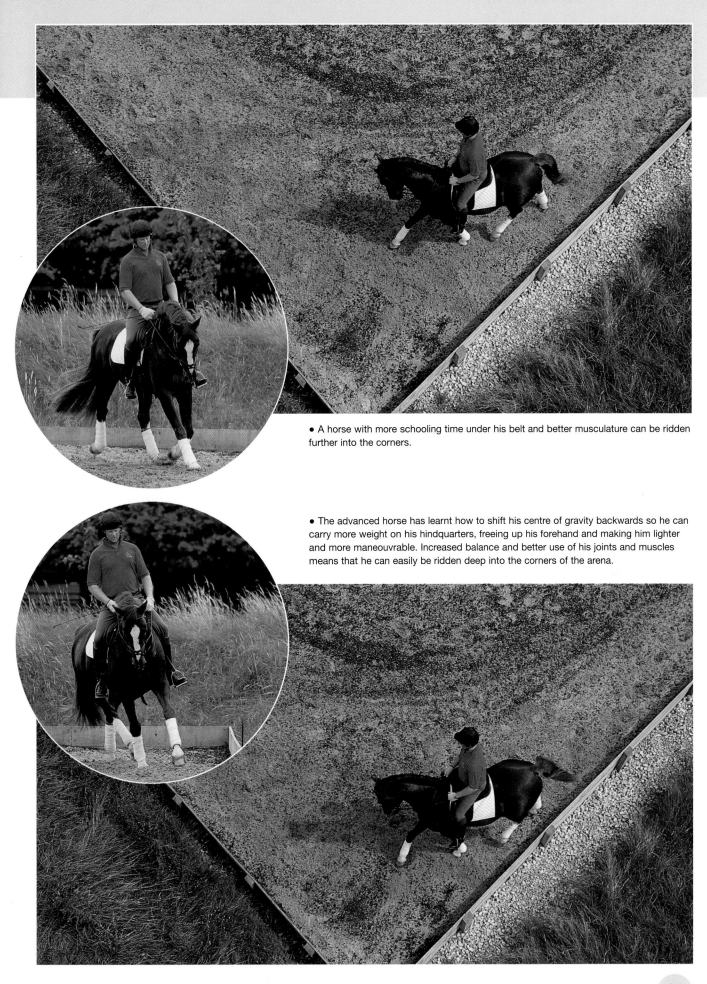

● A horse with more schooling time under his belt and better musculature can be ridden further into the corners.

● The advanced horse has learnt how to shift his centre of gravity backwards so he can carry more weight on his hindquarters, freeing up his forehand and making him lighter and more maneouvrable. Increased balance and better use of his joints and muscles means that he can easily be ridden deep into the corners of the arena.

Assessing your horse

By considering the questions here, you should get an idea of areas you need to work on with your horse and this will help you select suitable exercises from this book. First, decide how well schooled your horse is by thinking about the questions below:

- Does he turn equally well on both reins?
- Do his upward and downward transitions feel smooth in all paces?
- Does he respond immediately to my aids?
- Can I lengthen and shorten his stride easily in all paces?
- Can he maintain his balance and rhythm throughout changes of rein and speed?
- Can I ride him in an outline (see Outline, below)?
- What lateral work can we do?

OUTLINE

The outline is the shape that the horse makes when ridden. It will vary according to the horse's level of training and the rider's ability. In the early stages of training, when he hasn't developed the muscles needed to take more weight on his hindquarters (see Collection, p.14), he will work in a longer frame than that of more advanced horses. However, you should still aim to have him going forwards actively with sufficient impulsion so that he can undertake movements easily. He should also be accepting the bit and, therefore, be relaxed in the jaw.

An Alternative Approach

Another way of assessing your horse is to ask yourself:

What do I like and dislike about my horse?

It's human nature to do more of the things we enjoy, so the things we dislike about our horse, such as he's difficult to sit to, his left canter transition is tricky, he 'motorbikes' around corners, and so on, are often the areas we need to work on.

What do I enjoy about riding and why?

Concentrating on the aspects of riding you enjoy helps focus you on the positive benefits you can derive from schooling. As an example, if you enjoy cross-country jumping, consider how you could improve your performance. You might be able to take more direct routes if you knew you could keep your horse straight and balanced. If you are keen on show jumping think about the value of teaching your horse to lengthen and shorten his stride. You therefore have the option of choosing the number of strides eg when fences are at related distances to each other, to give your horse the best chance of jumping well.

What has changed in my riding in recent years? Has the change been for better or worse?

If you haven't had a lesson recently, it's likely that you've fallen into bad habits. The problem is that bad habits can feel so normal that you may not recognise them unless someone else points them out. Have you challenged yourself in the past few years or has your riding reached a plateau and stayed there? What new skills have you acquired? Are you more or less confident about jumping or competing? Taking a cold look at your riding will highlight areas where you need to seek help.

What has changed in my horse's training in recent years?

Have you schooled your horse regularly or not? Does he have a varied programme of activities? Or do you just hack around, without any schooling plan to keep him supple? Examine your horse's life honestly to pinpoint shortfalls and then use this book and a reputable instructor to work out a programme to help.

And, finally...

You may find it helpful to watch a video of you riding your horse: you should be able to see whether he can negotiate corners in balance or not, whether he falls in or out around circles, flexes his hocks, looks stiff in his back and so on.

Schooling sessions

The amount of schooling your horse receives during a week usually depends on the discipline you are interested in and the amount of time you have. Your horse's well-being is dependent on you providing variety and stimulation for him through his work, as well as creating a good balance between work and play, so even if you are planning to specialise in dressage, it's important not to overdo the training – he needs time at liberty and he will appreciate hacks out and jumping sessions, along with his flatwork.

Schooling sessions should not be overlong, especially if you are working with a young horse: 20–30 minutes is usually fine for a youngster. With any horse, finish the session on a good note.

WORKING OUT A TYPICAL SESSION

A schooling session can be divided into four phases:

• Warm up

• Work

• New work – introducing new manoeuvres (this phase may be omitted if either you or your horse are not working particularly well)

• Cool down

WARM UP/1 ▶

Allow some time for your horse to limber up, especially if he has come straight from his stable to the arena. Walk around on a loose rein for five or ten minutes, working on straight lines and curves rather than tight circles. You can include lots of directional changes, as you want your horse to be paying attention to you. Use this period to run through a checklist of your riding position and your objectives for the schooling session.

WARM UP/2 ▶

Take up a contact on the reins and start to warm up using walk, trot and canter. At each pace check that your horse is going forwards, straight and in a regular rhythm. When trotting use rising trot, riding him forward, but not pushing him out of his natural rhythm. Work him in a deep frame, keeping him moving actively forwards but allowing him to stretch his neck towards the contact and take the rein down, his back raised and his hindlegs coming under his body. Maintain impulsion and balance – he shouldn't be on the forehand. This stretches, warms and loosens the muscles over his neck and back so that they are prepared for work – this also minimises the risk of injury.

▲ WARM UP/3

Introduce canter, working initially in a forward seat with your weight out of the saddle to help the horse's back muscles. Check that he is listening and is responsive to you. Include school figures such as large circles and loops, and make sure you use all of the arena. As your horse's training advances, you can incorporate more lateral work in the warm-up period.

TIPS

You can see that this horse's trot is not yet active enough. We want the prints left by his hind feet to at least match those left by his forefeet, which is not yet happening.

WARM UP/4 ▶

Use frequent transitions to reduce tension in your horse – part of the purpose of the warm up. Spend as much time as necessary to get him relaxed – allow 20 minutes or even more if he needs it.

▼ REVISION WORK

The next stage is to go over work your horse already knows, such as circling, seeking to refine it and achieve some improvement during each session. Lots of little increments in skill result in a much more proficient horse and rider partnership. This part of your session may take 15 to 25 minutes.

▲ NEW WORK

This phase may be omitted if either you or your horse are not working particularly well.

If all has gone well so far, you can now teach your horse a new skill – here backing up. If he has been distracted or tense, however, or things are just not going too well, it's sensible to forego this until another day. Remember how you feel when learning something new (at college, when starting a new job): you need time to assimilate the information before putting it into practice. Your horse will be just the same, so don't expect perfection from him and do reward him for his efforts. As a rough guideline you may spend around 10 minutes on this aspect of your programme.

COOLING DOWN

Finish the new work on a good note and then start to cool down your horse. If he has found something difficult, it may be best to go back to some established work that he finds easy so that you can finish on a positive note.

• Trotting your horse in a deep frame (left), as you did for the warm up, helps to stretch and loosen the muscles.

• Move him around, working on large circles (top right).

• After a couple of minutes, come forward to walk and complete the session by walking around the arena on a loose rein, until your horse is cool (bottom right).

This cooling down period is just as important as the warming up section as your horse's muscles need to cool down gradually and his heart rate needs to return to its usual resting rate. If you fail to cool down properly, your horse could have sore, stiff muscles tomorrow.

TIPS FOR SUCCESSFUL SCHOOLING

- Take frequent breaks during a schooling session so your horse can relax and stretch. If you work him in an outline for too long, his muscles may ache (especially if he is unused to the work) and you'll only make him resistant. Allowing him a break to stretch also acts as a reward for him.

- If your horse has a problem with balance, try lungeing him. Done correctly, this will help him to establish his balance before he has to deal with the added problem of a rider. Lungeing also provides you with the opportunity of seeing how he moves.

- To give some structure to your long-term schooling, look at the levels of dressage tests to see when various movements are introduced. These will give you an idea of a logical progression for your training.

- Make sure that your horse is completely comfortable before you begin, otherwise you will achieve nothing. For example, stiffness through his back leads to poor transitions, which will affect all other movements.

- If you need to make a correction to your horse's way of going, do so, but immediately soften your hand and encourage him to go forwards (below).

- This horse is tilting his head to the right. The problem may well be due to the rider being stronger in that rein but she has to correct the horse and ask him to straighten up.

- Having made the correction the rider softens her hands and allows the horse forward. He must be rewarded for doing the right thing, otherwise he will have no incentive to learn.

FLEXING EXERCISE

If your horse takes the contact more on one rein than on the other, or is generally resistant in his jaw, try flexing him from side to side. This is not a sawing action that will result in him swinging his head one way and then the other. If your horse does start swinging his head, you are being too strong in the hand.

- To be straight (top left) a horse needs to take the contact evenly in both reins, but all horses are softer on one side than the other.

- You can soften a horse by flexing him first one way and then the other (bottom left). When you do this you just want to see the corner of his eye, you do not want to bend his head and neck around too far. Practise this by riding along one side of the arena with the horse flexing to the outside and then along the other side with him flexing to the inside. You can also practise flexing on circles.

- If the horse bends too much one way because you are too strong in the hand, you'll lose his quarters as they will swing away (right).

SEEKING A CONTACT

It's a good sign if your horse is wet in his mouth as it indicates that he has been seeking a contact with the bit.

35

Watch your position

Horses mirror their riders: if your posture is balanced, they can carry you easily and carry themselves in a good outline. Equally, if you have a postural problem, they will reflect this as they adapt themselves to deal with your problem. All riders have varying degrees of injuries, stresses and strains in their bodies that affect the way they sit on their horses.

As an Equine Muscle Release Therapy (EMRT) practitioner I am also required to train in the Bowen technique for humans, which is extremely useful in resolving many problems experienced by people, such as back pain, frozen shoulders, pelvic problems, knee injuries and so on. As part of our training we visited a riding centre where we assessed a particular horse and noted the way he carried himself. We then assessed the posture of the horse's owner and watched her ride. It was fascinating to see how the horse adapted his way of going to accommodate his owner's particular problems. What was even more interesting was seeing the horse ridden by two other people who had never previously ridden him. In each case, the horse quickly adapted his way of going according to the individual's postural carriage, shortening his stride and curling around in the completely opposite direction to what was 'normal' for him.

As horses react so quickly to the posture of whoever is riding them, it's mind-blowing to think how they must feel after years of carrying a rider who is out of balance, who is always collapsing their hip and so on. It's certainly a good reason to monitor your own riding position on a daily basis. Make use of photographs and videos to analyse your riding position as well.

• Our model is demonstrating a common fault here – you can see that her right shoulder is lower, which means that the whole of her right side will be collapsed.

● Twisting of the body is another common problem, especially when the rider is trying too hard to achieve a particular schooling movement. Riders whose horses are not very responsive to the aids often develop this habit.

Using an arena

To school your horse you'll need to ride a variety of school movements. It's much easier to ride these accurately if you do them in an arena or a marked out area. If you don't have access to a proper school, mark out a space in your field, perhaps using poles to indicate the boundaries. To work properly, your area needs to correspond to the systems of lettering and distance used in standard dressage arenas.

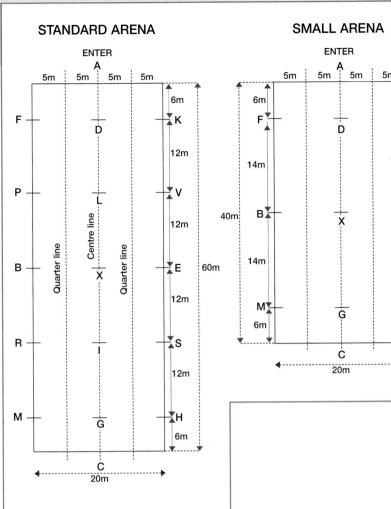

STANDARD ARENA

ENTER
A
5m 5m 5m 5m

F — D — K   6m
              12m
P — L — V   12m
    Centre line
B — X — E   12m   60m
    Quarter line Quarter line
R — I — S   12m
M — G — H   6m

C
20m

1m=3¼ft

SMALL ARENA

ENTER
A
5m 5m 5m 5m

6m
F — D — K
14m
B — X — E
40m
14m
M — G — H
6m

C
20m

There are two sizes of dressage arena in use: the large 20 metre by 60 metre arena and the smaller 20 metre by 40 metre arena. Each arena is divided lengthways by the centre line and then both halves of the school are further divided lengthways by the quarter lines. The letters are placed at set distances.

Familiarise yourself with the distances and letters so you can ride school figures accurately. It's important to realise, for instance, that when riding a 20-metre circle from A or C you need to go past the corner markers (F & K or M & H). In fact you need to go four metres down from the corner letters – before you turn across the school towards X. If you mistakenly turn at the markers, your circle will be more of an egg shape and certainly won't measure 20 metres! Get to know the reference points for circles and, if necessary, walk around the arena yourself so you know exactly where you are going when you ride. Mark out the points with cones at first. The diagrams on the right show the location of 15- and 20-metre circles.

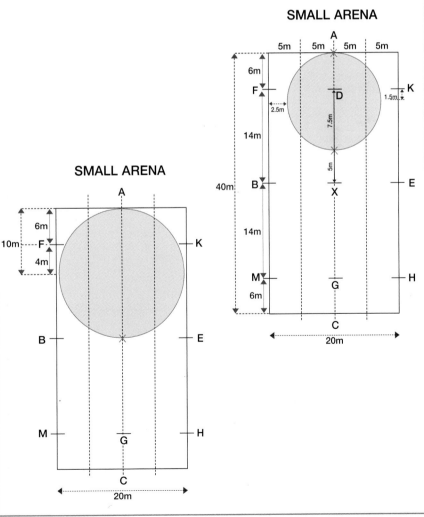

SMALL ARENA

A
6m
10m F — — K
4m

B — — E

M — — H

C
20m

SMALL ARENA

A
5m 5m 5m 5m

6m
F — D — K   1.5m
2.5m   7.5m
14m
40m   B — X — E
5m
14m
M — G — H
6m

C
20m

39

Riding in the arena

Once you are in the arena on your horse, you need to think ahead and prepare for each move. Riding along a long side requires you to keep him moving forwards and straight, so you need to be aware if he is drifting off line slightly. Consider whether he carries his quarters to the inside more on one rein than on the other.

Is he hugging the side of the arena for security? How balanced does he feel? Does he 'motorbike' around corners? Are you using a half-halt to rebalance him before he turns around the corner? Can you maintain the impulsion around a turn? There are so many things

▼ **TURNING AROSS A DIAGONAL**
Here the rider is making a turn off the right rein across the long diagonal.

• Use the corner to activate the hindquarters and thus maintain impulsion through the turn.

• Look across to where you want to be.

to think about – and you've only been in the arena five minutes! As, hopefully, you will have realised by now, schooling certainly isn't boring! If offers so much to occupy the mind as well as the body – 30 minutes can pass like lightning.

HALF-HALT

This is a re-balancing aid which is a barely visible combination of seat, legs and hands, used to increase a horse's attention and momentarily slow the pace before asking him to go forwards again. The effect is that his weight is transferred backwards so helping to engage the hindquarters (see also p.80).

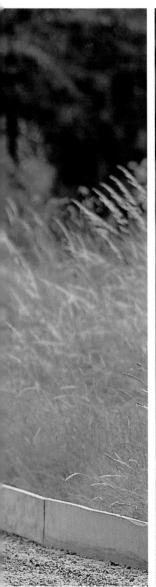

• With the turn on to the diagonal completed, now concentrate on keeping your horse forwards and straight.

Changing direction

Frequent changes of rein (direction) are needed throughout a schooling session. Apart from the fact that it would be very boring for both horse and rider to work constantly on one rein, equal work on both reins helps to produce a horse that is as ambidextrous and symmetrical as possible. Because the inside hindleg (for example, the offhind when the horse is on the right rein) takes more of the weight and shock absorption than the outside hindleg, changing the rein allows the hindlegs to rest alternately.

To change the rein effectively, the rider needs to consider the horse's balance and bend through the turns and his straightness in between. For example, this is the sequence when changing from the left rein across the diagonal from H to F:

- Before H the rider half-halts to rebalance the horse and maintain the impulsion because just after the turn there is a long straight path towards F.
- After H the horse needs to be as straight as possible in his spine to travel in a straight line towards F with balance and rhythm.
- The rider looks ahead and prepares because just before the F corner he needs to half-halt to rebalance the horse for the turn and he also has to allow for bending to the right.
- In rising trot the rider also has to change diagonals (see p.56) during this sequence – some people prefer to do this as they pass the X marker and others leave the change until just before the corner marker.

(see p.56)

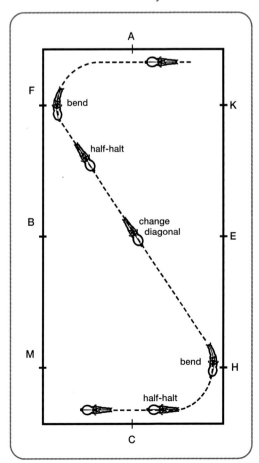

MAINTAINING STRAIGHTNESS

- If your horse finds it difficult to maintain his straightness for the long diagonal or is too onward-bound (moving with speed rather than impulsion), use this shorter diagonal, eg B to K

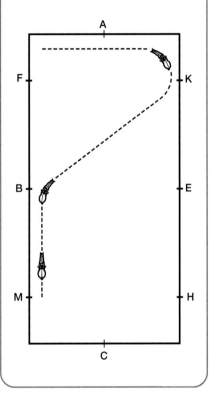

ROUTES TO CHANGE THE REIN

Here are just a few of the options for changing the rein. Make sure you use a selection of those that your horse can manage at his level of training:

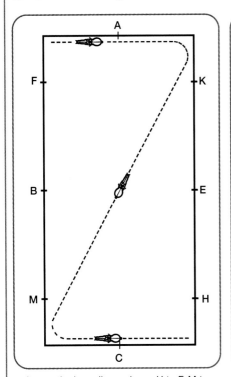

- Across the long diagonals, eg H to F, M to K, or vice versa.

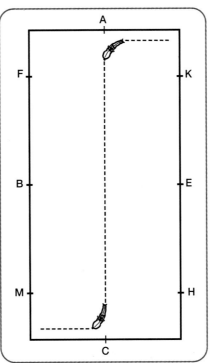

- Down the centre line, eg A to C. Take note of which rein you find this easiest on and remember it for when you enter the arena to do a dressage test.

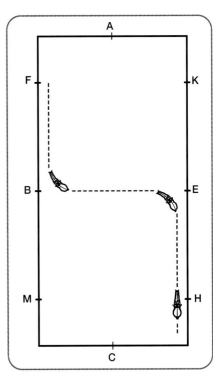

- Across the arena, eg E to B.

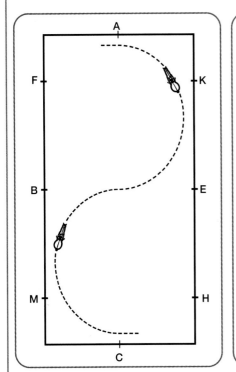

- By riding a half 20-metre circle from A to X and another half 20-metre circle from X to C.

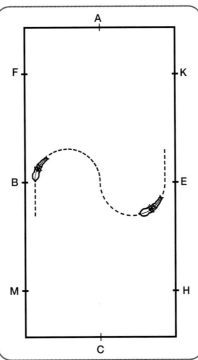

- By riding a half 10-metre circle from B to X and another from X to E.

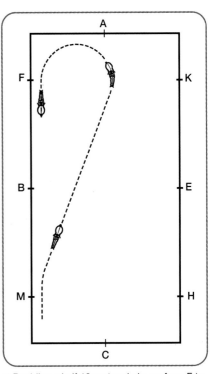

- By riding a half 10-metre circle, eg from F to X, and then inclining back to the track before M.

Crossing the arena from B to E

Always look ahead so that you are a couple of reference points ahead at any one time and be aware that when you are concentrating on an exercise, it's easy to get stuck on the same rein.

● Think ahead, preparing for the turn, by using a half-halt. Be aware of your own body position.

● Imagine that there is a line in the sand from B to E. Plan your turn so that your outside foot is directly over this line.

● Advance your inside hip slightly to tell your horse which way you want him to turn and invite him to do so with the inside rein. The inside hand is raised very slightly. Your inside leg acts at the girth to ask the inside hindleg to step under.

● Don't forget that your outside aids will also be helping the turn. The outside leg is behind the girth, ready to be used if the quarters swing out. The outside rein, if lowered and used along the neck, acts as a barrier and prevents the shoulder drifting out.

● Concentrate on keeping your horse straight, riding him in a tunnel formed by your legs and hands. Remember to change the diagonal.

● Ensure your rein contact is even and that your weight is in the middle of the saddle. Look ahead as it's only a short distance to the next marker and you have to prepare your horse for the turn.

● As you negotiate the turn and meet the track, you have to think about adjusting body weight and aids so…

● …that you can ride your horse forwards and straight, in good balance, along the long side of the arena.

Flatwork

Work on the flat is the key to enjoying your horse. In the early days of a horse's education his early lessons will focus on control and steering. As a horse's training progresses so his flatwork will help to develop his muscles, his suppleness, co-ordination and self-carriage. Throughout a horse's life it is important to continue his flatwork training so that he remains a responsive, obedient ride.

Although many exercises are performed in an arena you can include flatwork in your hacks – using transitions, performing turn on the forehand or haunches to open gates, using shoulder-in to go past hazards and so on. It should be enjoyable for your horse – for like us, horses learn best when they are relaxed and are enjoying the learning process.

The Paces: Walk

The horse's walk is a difficult pace to ride well because it has less natural momentum than the faster paces. It is a four-time movement – the sequence of footfalls is right hind, right fore, left hind, left fore – with the horse having at least two feet on the ground at any one time, and because there is no moment of suspension (when all four feet are off the ground), it is difficult to extend or collect it.

• If a horse is walking in a true four-time rhythm his fore foot will almost touch his hind foot as it comes forward and, together the legs will make a V-shape, which quickly disappears. However, this horse needs to be more relaxed and longer through his neck.

• Where there is no four-time rhythm there is a complete lack of a V-shape.

HOW DOES YOUR HORSE WALK?

Watch your horse walking and note how he moves. The strides should be equal and regular with the hind feet being put down in front of, or at least on, the tracks left by the front feet. Assess his walk. You should be able to answer yes to each of these questions:

• Does he take equal steps?

• Is he straight?

• Does he flex his hocks equally and raise his knees to the same height?

• Viewed from behind, does his bottom swing easily from side to side?

• Is his tail relaxed?

• Problems might be indicated by a tilted head, a dragging toe or a stiffness when viewed from behind.

• Previous schooling might have spoilt the way your horse moves (see Correcting a Ruined Walk, p.53): when assessing his walk consider his size and breeding. Does his walk stride suit him?

◀ Types of walk

MEDIUM WALK

This is the basic walking pace. Your horse should go forwards freely and energetically but calmly. Here, the rider is restricting the movement with her hands so that you can see how it affects the horse – he shortens his stride in front and overbends, bringing his head into his chest and dropping the bit.

FREE WALK

In free walk the horse goes forward, taking longer relaxed steps, stretching his neck down and elevating his back. The rider allows for this stretching by lengthening the reins but keeps a light contact with the mouth in order to achieve a free walk on a long rein (as opposed to no contact which would be free walk on a loose rein).

ADVANCED WALKS

Your horse can learn extended walk and collected walk once he has become very proficient in his schooling. In extended walk the steps are lengthened so that the horse covers as much ground as possible while still remaining on the bit. He may lengthen his outline a little. Collected walk is only suitable for advanced horses as it requires great engagement of the hindquarters and a lightening of the forehand. The steps are higher and cover less ground.

IMPROVING YOUR HORSE'S WALK

• If your horse has irregular walk steps, use ground poles to regulate his pace and to encourage him to use his hindquarters more. Working over poles also encourages a horse to lift and place each foot carefully. Start off with just one pole and work up to five. For walking, the distance between each pole is normally 90cm (3ft) but experiment to find the distance that best suits your horse.

• You can get your horse to take longer walk steps by using your legs alternately (left), in time with his movement. As he walks along you should be able to feel your horse's belly swinging from side to side – when his belly swings away from your leg, his corresponding hindleg is being lifted off the ground and this is the time when you can influence it most. Just as you feel the belly swing away from your leg, apply your leg aid, using your calf, and you will encourage his hindleg to come further under his body. The timing of your aid is crucial. If you apply it when the horse's belly is swinging into your leg, then his hindleg is being put on to the ground and you cannot influence it. You can see (here) that the near hind is just coming off the ground. If the rider uses her left leg now she can encourage the near hind to come further under the horse's body.

• If your horse finds it difficult to stretch in free walk (right), ride plenty of changes of direction, such as on a serpentine or on adjoining 10-metre circles, concentrating on flexing the horse to the inside. This should help to loosen his muscles so he can stretch down.

• Lazy horses that do not track up in walk can be encouraged to use themselves more through lateral work (see pp.103–117) so that they step under themselves more. Lateral work such as shoulder-in (far right) is also good for horses that tend to hurry when they walk. Shoulder-in brings the horse's forehand off the track by an angle of about 30 degrees so the inside hindleg is in line with the outside fore-leg. The exercise helps the horse to accept the rider's leg rather than running away from the aids.

• The transition from free walk on a long rein to medium walk may cause problems if the horse starts to anticipate the transition and breaks into trot as he feels the reins being shortened. If your horse does this, ride 10-metre circles in medium walk, moving from one circle to another by using a short period of free walk on a long rein. This exercise will accustom your horse to you lengthening and shortening the reins. If you do it across the long diagonals you can alternate the direction as well.

• A horse with an irregular walk rhythm may be helped by being asked to slow down, but some horses benefit from being asked to go forward in a faster tempo: experiment to find which seems to help your horse.

TIPS TO HELP YOUR HORSE'S WALK

- Walk is the easiest pace to ruin, so try not to interfere with a young horse's walk unless absolutely necessary (see Corrrecting a Ruined Walk, opposite).

- Giving your horse breaks by using free walk helps to loosen the muscles in his neck and back.

- Tune in to your horse's movement: as he walks along, use your seatbones to try to identify which hindleg is being picked up (below left). When the left hindleg is on the ground, the horse's left hip is higher and you should feel your left seatbone being raised slightly. Call out left, right, as you feel the movement and ask a friend to check whether you are correct.

- Be aware of your rein contact: you do not want to restrict your horse's forward movement.

- All riders have one side that is stronger than the other – from this overhead shot (below) you can see that this rider is stronger on her left side, so she needs to be careful not to restrict the horse on this side.

- When you ride on roads, you can hear your horse's footfalls, so use the opportunity to check the regularity of his pace. A break in the rhythm could be due to stiffness or tension (see EMRT in Useful Addresses).

- Appropriate work in trot and canter, such as suppling exercises, lengthening and shortening and lateral work (all covered in this book), will have beneficial effects on your horse's walk.

CORRECTING A RUINED WALK

If a horse has been restricted and he shuffles along rather than striding out freely you can encourage him to walk out properly by 'swinging' him along. This is a technique Michael Peace (behaviourist and trainer, pictured left) uses to encourage stuffy horses to go forward and to generally free-up horses that are restricted in their paces. It can be used in walk, trot and canter.

Use your leg aids alternately, in tune with the horse's stride – as you feel his belly swing away from your leg, use your leg on that side. The horse's hindleg is just about to leave the ground at this point, so you can influence how far it goes if you time your aid correctly. As you use your left leg, take the right rein several inches out to the side. As you use your right leg, take the left rein out. Be careful to take the rein out – as if you are using an open rein – rather than backwards. The hand aids are initially quite exaggerated so that you are swinging your arms from side to side. Keep the reins loose and have a light contact. As you 'swing' the horse along, you will find that he relaxes and starts to open up his stride.

The Paces: Trot

Trot is a two-time movement with the horse's legs moving in diagonal pairs, so the near hind moves with the off fore, and the off hind with the near fore. As the horse springs from one pair of legs to the other, there is a moment of suspension when all four legs are off the ground.

HOW DOES YOUR HORSE TROT?

Your horse should look as if he is propelling himself forward from the hindlegs, rather than dragging himself forward with his forelegs. Propulsion from behind means that the horse is better balanced and will be able to maintain a steady rhythm and outline throughout any exercise you ask him to do. When a horse is really using his hindlegs you will see a V-shape made by his legs (top, right) and he should be flexing his knees and hocks (below, right).

- If the 1,2, 1,2 count for a trot is not rhythmical it could be that the horse is lame.
- Sometimes what should be one beat for a diagonal pair of legs is heard as two separate beats. This may be because the horse is very heavy on his shoulders or lazy in his hindlegs, in which case lots of transitions will help to lighten his forehand, and lengthening and shortening the trot will activate his hindlegs.

DIAGONALS

- You can assist your horse's balance by riding on the correct diagonal in trot. Horses find it easier to carry their riders if the rider's weight is in the saddle when the horse's inside hindleg is on the ground. For instance, if you are riding on the right rein, you should sit in the saddle as the horse's off hind is on the ground. As the legs work in diagonal pairs at trot this means that his near fore is also on the ground (left). You can see the near fore coming to ground by glancing down at the horse's near shoulder and so can time your 'sit' beat. Learn to feel when you are on the correct diagonal rather than glancing down every time.

- To change diagonals 'sit' for two beats. In the school, change the diagonal every time you change rein; when hacking or riding on the trail, it's good practice to change diagonals frequently, otherwise your horse will become one-sided and stiff. Horses that are stiff often 'throw' their riders on to their most comfortable diagonal so you need to be aware of this. Tell-tale signs of a stiff horse are uneven muscle development and crookedness. Riders also have a diagonal they favour.

Types of trot

WORKING TROT

This is your everyday trot. It should be energetic, with a consistent rhythm and tempo, so that when you ride around the arena you can feel no difference as you negotiate both long and short sides. In working trot the horse goes forward in balance, taking even, elastic steps and bending his hock joints.

MEDIUM TROT

This requires greater activity from the hindquarters so that the horse's stride is longer than in working trot and the moment of suspension is longer.

EXTENDED TROT

This movement is a progression from medium trot, with the horse taking longer strides, covering as much ground as possible.

COLLECTED TROT

As with the collected walk (p.49), collected trot is for advanced schooling. It involves the horse taking short, elevated steps with his hindquarters engaged and his frame shortened.

IMPROVING YOUR HORSE'S TROT

- Get more energy into your horse's trot by riding over trotting poles (left). The distances between poles will vary according to your horse's stride length but, for example, for a 16hh horse start with a separation of 1.4m (4½ft). You can see from the side-on view (below) how much lift the exercise has given to this horse's trot.

- Once your horse is happy working over poles, raise alternate ends of the poles about 5cm (2in) off the ground so he has to work harder and flex his joints more. Then you can progress to having each pole raised 5cm (2in) along its length, building up to no more than 15cm (6in) in gradual stages. Don't overdo this exercise, as it is really hard work for a horse.

- Transitions to and from trot will encourage your horse to move off by pushing from his hindquarters (left) rather than being on the fore-hand.

- Irregular steps with a hindleg could indicate that the horse is lazy or weak on that leg. There may also be a muscular problem. Do the following exercise to strengthen a weak hindleg. For example, if the near hind is weak, work on the right rein so that the weak leg is to the outside of the arena. Use counter bend for a couple of strides – bend your horse's head to the left and use the left leg behind the girth to push the hindquarters to the right, so that the near hind has to step under the body more. Now straighten and ride forwards. Repeat this several times in a lesson, interspersing it among other exercises.

TIPS FOR TROT

- Trot has the same sequence of footfalls on each rein, so it's easy to change direction and bend without causing too much disruption (right). Aim to flow from one exercise to another, using frequent changes of rein so that your horse's body is worked equally on each side.

- The symmetrical movement of the trot makes it a good schooling pace. It's the easiest pace for establishing rhythm.

- Because of its natural spring, trot is an effective pace for doing lateral work. You can see how this horse is stepping under with his hindleg (left).

- For the lower levels of dressage test, trot may be performed rising or sitting. However, as you progress up the levels, sitting trot is specified. To sit well to the trot takes practice. If you find it difficult, don't try to do it for long periods. This is because the more you try, the more uncomfortable and tense you'll become and the harder it will be to sit softly and absorb the movement. Sit for a few strides, then resume rising and repeat the procedure. Gradually build up the number of sitting trot strides.

- It's difficult to sit to the trot if you collapse forwards. This closes your hip joint so you can't absorb your horse's movement.

LUNGE LESSONS ARE GOOD FOR YOU

A good riding position is vitally important and is something that all riders strive for. However, unless you have regular tuition it is easy to slip into bad habits and soon positional defects such as leaning forward or having your legs too far forward feel normal. To overcome such problems it is worth investing in some lunge lessons. A good instructor and good lunge horse will be needed if you are to make good progress. In addition to working on your overall position lunge lessons are useful for developing your balance and confidence. Skills such as sitting to the trot can also be practised.

The Paces: Canter

Canter is a three-time pace with a moment of suspension. If the horse is cantering on the right rein, the sequence of footfalls will be near hind, then off hind and near fore together as a diagonal pair, then off fore, followed by a moment of suspension before the cycle starts again. The off fore, which completes this sequence, is known as the leading leg. The rocking sensation of the canter is produced because the horse lowers and raises his head throughout the footfall sequence, as his forehand rises and lowers.

HOW DOES YOUR HORSE CANTER?

• Aim for regular strides with good rhythm and balance (left). The joints of the hindlegs should be flexed and each foot should be placed on the ground firmly and without hesitation.

• In canter your horse should be straight, with his shoulders directly in front of the hindquarters (right).

• If your horse carries his hind-quarters to one side, straighten him by moving the front end over (far right). To mobilise the shoulders, practise making transitions along the long side of the school, going from straight to shoulder-fore position (see p.108) and then straight again.

◀ Types of canter
WORKING CANTER

This is the initial schooling pace and is between medium and collected canter. The horse must go forwards in balance and with light, even strides, the propulsive power being provided by his active hindquarters.

◀ MEDIUM CANTER

In this, the next step up from working canter, the horse is expected to show longer strides and greater impulsion.

◀ EXTENDED CANTER

Without losing any rhythm or balance, the horse lengthens his stride into extended canter to cover as much ground as possible while remaining light and on the bit.

COLLECTED CANTER ▶

The stride for collected canter is the shortest of any of the canters – the horse's hindquarters are engaged and the forehand is light. The whole appearance of this pace is of lightness and mobility.

◀ COUNTER CANTER

In a true right canter on a right rein the horse's off fore is the leading leg and is on the inside of the circle. In counter canter the horse is asked to lead with his outside foreleg, so on a circle to the right, for example, he would canter with the left lead and with the bend over this leading leg. Counter canter is a specific exercise that is helpful in improving suppleness in the horse's shoulders and back and also assists in engaging the hindquarters. It is entirely different to a disunited canter – this is an incorrect movement and occurs when the forehand and hindquarters are on different leads. In these pictures you can see the horse coming off the track in counter canter (above) – note how he is bent to the left over the leading leg (left).

Achieving strike-off

The easiest time to attempt a transition into canter is as you come into a corner of the arena or, on a 20-metre circle, as you cross over the centre line. Use the inside rein to flex the horse's head to the inside, and the outside rein to control the gait. Your outside leg should be behind the girth (one hand's width) and this leg instigates the first beat. At the same time the inside leg is on the girth and is responsible for sending the horse forward. The action of the inside leg is to give a little inwards nudge.

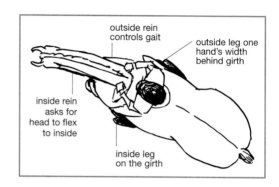

outside rein controls gait

outside leg one hand's width behind girth

inside rein asks for head to flex to inside

inside leg on the girth

▲ RESISTANCE

This horse is being resistant as he is asked to strike-off into canter. If this happens to you, calmly bring your horse forward to trot again, activate the hindquarters by riding a 10-metre circle close to a corner and then ask for the transition again as you come into the corner.

This is a better strike-off into ▶ canter.

IMPROVING YOUR HORSE'S CANTER

• The canter should have a distinct three-time beat but if your horse is too much on the forehand, the diagonal pair of legs can split so that the foreleg comes to the ground before the hindleg. Incorporate lots of transitions into your schooling to lighten his forehand – this work can be done on the lunge as well as under saddle. Lengthening and shortening the stride also helps to engage the hindquarters and free the forehand.

• If your horse is crooked, check that you haven't asked for too much bend in the neck. If you can see more than just the corner of his inside eye, you have too much bend.

• Stop cantering if your horse starts to go hollow, raising his head and dipping and tensing his back. If he often rushes and his canter is difficult to sit to, he will have a tendency to be hollow, too. Return to a slower pace and ask him to round again, relaxing his jaw and accepting the bit and stepping under with his hindlegs, before moving into a faster pace. Working in a hollow outline (below) can strain your horse's muscles.

TIPS FOR IMPROVING THE CANTER

- If the canter looks as if the nearside fore and hindlegs are moving together and the offside fore and hind legs are moving together, it may be because your horse is stiff in his back and neck. Seek advice from a qualified and recommended therapist, such as a physiotherapist, chiropractor or EMRT therapist. Ask your vet if he knows of a local therapist with a good reputation.

- Trying to shorten a horse's canter stride before he is strong enough to do this results in the diagonal pair of legs splitting, with the hindleg hitting the ground first. You can tell whether your horse should be strong enough by looking at his musculature which should be evenly proportioned. If his hindquarters look considerably smaller than his forehand then he will not be ready for shortening.

- Crookedness is the cause of many canter problems – use shoulder-in position (see p.108) to help straighten a horse.

- In canter there is an undulating movement as the horse's forehand lowers and rises. As a result, his head appears to nod. If it nods excessively, the culprit is often a lack of impulsion, in which case you need to ride him forward strongly (below).

A canter exercise

• Cantering across the diagonal and preparing to give and retake the rein. The judges will be looking for the horse to maintain the correct sequence of steps throughout this exercise.

• The rider gives the rein, stretching his hands forward.

Giving and retaking the reins

Some dressage tests require the rider to 'give and retake' the reins in canter – a test of balance for both horse and rider. The aim is to show that the horse is carrying himself and is not going to fall into trot the second the rider stops holding him together. It should also show that his training has been correct in that he can stay straight. The whole movement should be one continuous fluid exercise: without leaning forward, the rider gradually releases the rein contact for a few strides and then gradually retakes it; the horse reaches forward slightly for the bit but otherwise remains in the same outline. The giving of the rein need only be for a stride or two. In a test, you will be marked down if your horse is crooked or deviates from the line. The exercise may be ridden across the diagonal, along a long side or on a circle and your horse is expected to follow the prescribed line as you give the rein. Any loss of balance will also be marked down, as will an increase in speed, or the horse falling into trot. Resistance to you retaking the rein also tells the judge that your preparation for this movement has been lacking.

• You can see that there is slack in the rein.

• This is an example of how not to do it – the rider is just locking his elbows and is not actually giving the rein.

GIVING AND RETAKING THE REIN TIPS

• You can use this exercise in trot and canter during your everyday schooling to test your horse's self-carriage. You can give and retake just one rein, such as the inside rein when riding a circle, which will test whether you have sufficient control with the outside rein. Giving the rein also makes the horse carry himself rather than lean on your hands (below).

• If your horse has problems with this exercise you will need to work more on his acceptance of the aids and engagement of the hindquarters, by using transitions, both direct and progressive (see pp.70–77), and lateral movements. Straightness, rhythm, suppleness and balance are key elements in his schooling programme and need re-evaluating regularly. It is often easier to start this exercise on a circle than a straight line, as this makes it easier to keep the horse balanced.

• Check your own position as well. It's tempting to lean forward as you give the rein but this only puts more weight on your horse's forehand. Accustom your horse to the feel of you breaking the contact with his mouth, as losing the security of your contact may initially worry him.

• This exercise will also reveal other possible problems, which you can then work on. For instance, your horse may snatch the rein away from you, which indicates that you have probably been too strong in the rein and holding him together. Think about the three-time rhythm of the pace as it is important this is maintained throughout the exercise.

Upward transitions

Transitions are changes of pace, such as from halt to walk, and changes within a pace, such as from working trot to medium trot. They can also occur as changes from movement to movement, such as a leg yield into a lengthening of stride. A progressive transition is where the horse moves through a pace, such as from walk to trot. However, if an intermediate pace is by-passed, asking the horse to go from walk into canter for example, this is known as a direct transition.

Transitions are extremely important to your horse's schooling. They improve his way of going by helping to increase his suppleness longitudinally and by engaging his hindquarters. They also help with his balance, as well as maintaining his interest when he works.

Transitions are included in dressage tests as, when accurate and well-ridden, they are proof of a well-schooled horse and a co-ordinated rider. Aim to make yours fluid and smooth but distinct. The last step of one pace and the first step of the next should be as good as all the other preceding and succeeding steps. Remember this so that you avoid allowing your horse to amble into transitions.

▼ UPWARD TRANSITION

Good preparation is vital if you are to make a good transition, whether it's upwards or downwards. Use one or more half-halts to warn the horse that you are about to ride a transition, as you need him to be attentive. The half-halt will also improve his balance and impulsion in preparation for the transition.

Be aware of the balance between your hand and leg aids as you ask for the upward transition – you don't want to have too strong a rein contact as you use your legs. Your horse must respect your aids: if he doesn't obey your legs at the first request, back up the aid with a tap of the whip behind your leg. As soon as he responds to the leg aids release them – remember that he should stay in the gait you've requested without you continually having to tell him to stay there. Nagging away with the legs tends to produce a horse that is 'dead' to the aids and is very hard work!

Upward transitions encourage your horse to use his hindquarters to greater effect and help to improve his balance. Your horse's neck is his main re-balancing mechanism and is a good indicator during a transition – if you see it stiffen and feel him hollow against you, you know that he is re-balancing himself. This might be because his balance is lacking or because you did not prepare him adequately for the transition.

Downward transitions

It's more difficult to keep the balance, activity in the hindlegs and impulsion for a downward transition, than it is for an upward transition. You must use your seat, legs and hands to achieve a fluid shift down into a slower gear. Your legs need to be closed around your horse to help keep his hindlegs active and to encourage him to step well under his body. If, for instance, you are moving from a trot to a walk, imagine his hindlegs taking one more trot step than the front legs. Get your horse's attention prior to the transition by using a half-halt and then, as you ask for the downward transition, contain the energy by closing your hands so that they are no longer allowing the momentum forward. Be prepared to allow with your hands – opening your fingers to give the contact a fraction – as the horse

• On the right rein in canter, the leading leg is the off fore and you can see here that it is about to come forward – the diagonal pair of off hind and near fore have just hit the ground – this will be followed by a moment of suspension before the whole cycle starts again (see p.60), which is an opportune time for a rider to ask for a downward transition.

• By retarding the movement with his seat and keeping his legs closed, John is able to interrrupt the canter cycle without Rio resisting. This also avoids the common problem in downward transitions – too great a use of the hand.

• This is a better trot stride although the horse is tilting his head a little to the inside.

• John corrects and guides Rio onto the next exercise – a circle.

changes gear downwards, otherwise the first step of the new pace could be restricted.

The weight aids should be used before leg and hand aids. However, there seem to be lots of different interpretations on the use of the seat (see box).

THE SEAT AID

Few instructors can explain clearly how to use the seat – employing a variety of terms such as brace the back, 'still' the seat, squeeze the buttocks together, stop following the movement and push the stomach forward. The most effective and logical explanation I have had was from respected teacher Heather Moffett. She asked me to sit on a hard chair and then to tighten my buttock muscles – as you do this your upper thigh muscles tighten and you can feel yourself rising up off the chair slightly. She explained that I was not rising off the chair in fact, but that my skeleton was being raised. When a rider does this on a horse, the horse feels a lightening in the saddle, which allows his back to come up underneath the rider. A horse used to feeling the rider's seatbones moving in time with his own movement, will notice when the movement suddenly stops as the rider tightens their seat and thigh muscles, and will slow down too. I have found this technique to work very well, even with young horses that have just been started.

• Riding a transition in this way makes for a more even change of pace – the horse is now in trot (look at the near hind and off fore) although there is a momentary hiccup with balance and he is a little on the forehand.

• Riding a half-halt helps him re-balance.

• As a result of the correction and the move onto the circle, the trot now has better steps and balance – and all this has happened in just a few seconds.

• Be aware of your posture during downward transitions – sit up, look up and keep your shoulders open and relaxed. Stay relaxed in your seat.

Direct transitions

When your horse shows good balance and rhythm through progressive transitions you can move on to the more difficult direct transitions, such as trot to halt or walk to canter.

For the upward transition of walk to canter you need to have plenty of energy in the walk before you move into canter. You can also make use of a 10-metre circle to ensure your horse has correct bend – his spine follows the line he is travelling on – and that he is using his hindlegs efficiently. Plan ahead so that he is in a good place for a canter strike-off, and time your aids carefully. Your outside leg will be behind the girth and the inside leg on the girth ready to give a friendly nudge as you feel his inside foreleg come

TROT TO HALT TRANSITION ▶

The rider aims for an active trot, with the horse thinking and moving forwards freely (top right).

He uses his seat to slow the movement (top centre), keeping his legs around the horse's body so that the hindlegs are encouraged to step under the body. The rider's hands contain the energy instead of yielding and allowing (top far right).

There is a walk step (below right) …

… and the rider uses his seat again to achieve (below centre) …

… halt. Note how the horse has maintained a round outline (below far right).

SIMPLE CHANGES OF REIN

Once your horse can execute direct transitions you can incorporate them into other exercises. A simple change of rein is achieved by riding two circles to give a figure of eight. Canter one circle, coming forward to walk for several strides at X and then ask for a canter strike-off on the other rein.

to the ground. At this point you know that the outside hind will be just leaving the ground so, if your timing is right, your horse should make a clean transition. Don't forget that once in canter you can use half-halts if necessary to re-balance him.

To make a downward transition from canter to walk, work on a 20-metre circle, aiming for a slow but energetic canter. You can decrease the circle size slightly to help slow your horse down. Keep your legs on to support him but ask for walk with your seat and your hands. Use the reins in a squeeze and release manner, rather than maintaining a continual pull, which will only encourage your horse to pull against you.

Spiralling in

If your horse has trouble keeping the bend to the inside during a direct transition into canter, work in an active walk on a 20-metre circle and gradually spiral in so that the circle becomes smaller, then gradually spiral out again, using your inside leg to push him out onto a larger circle.

Be aware of your horse's balance and only go as far as his training will allow. Repeat this spiralling in and out several times until he is bending softly and correctly. Then, as you spiral out again and reach the outer limits of the circle, ask for the direct transition into canter. Use the inside rein to maintain the bend to the inside. It's particularly important to remember to repeat the spiralling exercise on both reins, otherwise one of your horse's hindlegs will be more developed than the other.

Leg yield to canter strike-off

Another useful exercise to encourage the horse to use his hindlegs actively is to leg yield from the centre or quarter lines to a corner and then ask for a canter strike-off as you reach the corner. Again make sure you do this exercise on both reins so both hindlegs are worked equally.

Transitions within a pace

Transitions can also be performed within the same pace, for instance asking your horse to move from working to medium trot and back again. Refer to the information on lengthening and shortening strides on pp.84–89.

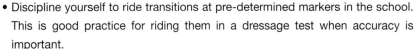

TIPS FOR GOOD TRANSITIONS

- For your horse's transitions to be smooth and co-ordinated he needs you to think ahead, prepare you both for the change and give smooth, clear aids.

- Aim to keep your horse round and relaxed during transitions. If he is stiffening against you beforehand, the problem will only become worse during the transition.

- Ride as many different horses as you can, working especially on transitions. Each horse can teach you something!

- Check you aren't making it difficult for your horse to make the direct transition into canter by pulling on the inside rein, which will effectively block his movement and interrupt his balance. If you are, train yourself out of the habit by taking your inside hand forward towards the horse's mouth so that there is a little slack in the inside rein.

- Discipline yourself to ride transitions at pre-determined markers in the school. This is good practice for riding them in a dressage test when accuracy is important.

Halt

In halt a horse should stand square with his weight evenly distributed on all four feet, with the front and hind pairs of legs being level with each other. He should be immobile but attentive to his rider and ready to move off at the slightest indication. The outline of the horse will depend upon his level of training with the more advanced horses showing greater engagement of the quarters and elevation of the forehand.

Halts need to be practised frequently, as an excellent halt can only be achieved through correct and systematic training. Preparation is the key: you must decide where to ride a halt, prepare yourself and the horse for the transition and then ride it purposefully to obtain a smooth square halt. To ride forwards from a halt, ensure your horse is in a suitable outline for his level of training and determine the pace at which you wish to proceed. Then you can apply your leg aids while also allowing with your hands for the forward movement to obtain a clear and active transition.

TIPS

- Ride your horse forwards into halt otherwise he will leave his hindlegs trailing and hollow his back. He may well lean on your hands. Maintain a good posture into the halt and keep the rein and leg contact. By keeping the leg contact you can also feel if he is wavering off line and can quickly correct the fault.

- If your horse does not stand square, ask him to move forwards, never backwards, in order to effect an improvement. Learn to feel which leg is out of line, rather than looking down to check.

▲ HALT
Horses have to be trained to halt square, and riders have to develop the feel for where their horses' legs are positioned underneath them.

◀ From a square halt, in good balance, it is much easier to make a good upward transition.

TROUBLESHOOTING

- If your horse trails his quarters out behind in halt, it will be impossible for him to move off easily into the next pace. Work on engaging his hindquarters through transitions and lateral work, such as turn on the forehand.

- Crookedness is another common fault in halt. Give yourself guidelines by asking your horse to halt between two poles laid on the ground. If he is constantly crooked ask someone to check your seat and use of the aids – if you are sitting crookedly or applying the aids stronger on one side then your horse won't be able to remain straight.

- **Above:** This horse is resisting into halt – his head is raised which means he hollows his back. Both he and the rider will be feeling uncomfortable.

- **Left:** In pic A the horse is falling to his right in halt. The rider therefore positions the horse slightly to his left – note the rider's shoulder position and the horse's forelegs in pic B.

Half-halt

A valuable tool in the rider's kit, the half-halt is a barely visible signal given to the horse through the co-ordinated action of seat, legs and hands. It is in effect a slowing of pace, but just before the horse drops to a lower pace, he is asked to move forward again. It should be a quick, tactful action that results in the horse increasing his attention and shifting his weight towards his hindquarters, therefore improving his balance. It is used to prepare a horse for a movement, such as turning or making a transition, to help him balance, before a jump for example, and to gain his attention, such as when out hacking.

To perform a half-halt you need to first check your own position and then within a fraction of a second use seat, legs and hands aids in that order. Taking a pull on the reins alone is not a half-halt. In order to help the horse re-balance you have to use all the aids.

• This horse is a little on the forehand (above) and is not really carrying his weight behind.

The rider sits taller and keeps both legs around the horse to maintain the energy and then closes the hand for a stride to give the half-halt (see main photograph opposite), making the horse wait and re-balance himself.

As a result an improved balance is obtained (below), with the horse carrying more weight on the hindleg and being more 'up' and relaxed in the forehand.

Riding a half-halt

To gain a feel for this movement, ride your horse on a circle in working trot, working on transitions. Then move on to 'almost' transitions – for example, where you ask your horse to almost walk but before he does you push him on again in trot.

Through these 'almost' transitions you can learn about the balance of seat, legs and hands and feel how your horse starts to engage his hindquarters. In this way, you can start to bring him together, a first step towards collection.

Initially, the half-halt will be a steadying aid to help your control and your horse's balance. However, as you become more co-ordinated and proficient in its use so you can encourage him to bring his hindquarters underneath him more and use himself more, giving a shorter but more elevated stride.

TIPS

- Ensure you use your rein contact well: you should not have a hard dead feel on the reins but be able to close your hand and then ease the contact by opening your fingers.

- Beware of giving away the rein (releasing the contact) because if you do the effect of the half-halt will be lost.

Rein back

This is a useful lesson to teach your horse at an early stage as there are bound to be occasions when you need to ask him to go backwards, such as when opening and shutting gates if there is no room to turn around properly. In such cases, it is very helpful if your horse knows how to move backwards calmly.

To teach your horse rein back, you should be able to ride transitions well, co-ordinating your aids to achieve a fluent upward or downward change of pace. In addition, you need to ride halts well and should be aware of your horse's balance and sequence of footfalls.

• In a rein back the horse moves his legs almost simultaneously in diagonal pairs, remaining straight in his body and his steps. From the ground, you should see his feet clearly being lifted and moved and taking even steps. He should maintain a good outline and balance. When the rein back is finished, he should move forwards willingly.

TIPS

- If your horse drags his feet or takes small steps this could be due to stiffness or resistance.

- Do not rein back if your horse hollows his outline (left) as this makes it difficult for him to do as you ask. Ride forward, re-establish a round outline and try again.

- Start off by asking for just one step at a time.

- Always ride your horse forward if he gets agitated with this exercise. You may need to teach the movement from the ground first.

▼ RIDING A REIN BACK

Ride forward to a square, balanced halt, keeping your horse on the aids. Close your legs around him as if you are asking him to step forward, but do not allow him to do so, gently restraining him, then ease your leg contact – as he cannot step forward he should step back (far left). If your horse doesn't understand what you are asking, ask someone on the ground to place a hand on his chest and encourage him to step back as you give the aids.

Your legs control the speed and number of steps backwards (centre and left). When you want to go forwards again, apply the leg aids but allow with your hands so that your horse can move forward.

Lengthened and shortened strides

The lower levels of dressage tests include working trot and working canter, and within these two gaits a rider is expected to show some lengthening of their horse's stride. This lengthening is clearly distinct from the longer length of stride shown in medium trot or canter or extended trot or canter. In working trot and working canter, the horse's centre of gravity tends to be towards the forehand and the lengthening of the stride in both these gaits does not alter this fact, whereas in medium and extended work, the horse's centre of gravity is shifted backwards as he has been trained to take more weight on the hindquarters.

When a horse lengthens his stride he keeps the same rhythm of the working gait, be it trot or canter, but elongates his stride and frame; as a result he covers more ground with each stride. How much lengthening he can achieve depends on his training and development.

So when should you start asking a horse to lengthen his strides?

Your horse needs to be established in working trot and canter. By this I mean that he is able to maintain his balance and rhythm and is responsive to your aids (he immediately responds to an instruction to go forwards). If these criteria are fulfilled then it is worth introducing lengthened strides, as they are a great aid to suppleness. From the purely physical point of view, lengthening and shortening a horse's stride makes him much more athletic so he can get himself out of trouble much more easily. This ability is valuable, especially for showjumpers and event horses that have to be able to adjust to all kinds of distances.

Riding shortened and lengthened strides

There are two parts to this exercise – shortening the stride and then lengthening it. Although it takes a long time to build a horse's muscles so that he can become truly collected, there is no reason why you cannot work towards collection. This will help your horse to use his hindquarters more effectively.

When you ask for lengthened strides don't be over ambitious – just a few strides is fine otherwise you run the risk of your horse losing his balance. Choose two markers to act as reference points for the start and finish of your exercise, for example H to E (see p.39). Ride along the long side of the arena in your normal working trot, counting out the number of strides between your two markers. (This is a relatively short distance but it is better to get two good strides than eight poor ones.)

START ON THE STRAIGHT

Although lengthened strides can be ridden on circles, it's easier to start off on straight lines. On a circle the horse has the added strain of his inside hindleg having to work harder and the rider also has to keep the horse in the correct bend. It is, therefore, more difficult for both horse and rider to start on a circle.

▼ SHORTENING

Now ride between your two markers, aiming to shorten your horse's stride. Your legs will be asking the horse to use his hindquarters more but your hands need to catch this energy rather than allow it forward, as you would do normally for a working trot. However, it's important that you keep your hands soft because pulling hands will only result in your horse hollowing against you. Count the number of strides. When you reach E return to working trot.

• The trot is active with the horse thinking forwards and moving freely forwards.

• To achieve a change to a slower trot, the rider slows the tempo of his sit, rise, sit, rise motion. His hands are also less yielding.

• The rider's legs are still keeping the horse stepping underneath himself.

• As this shortening of the stride has been brought about primarily through the seat aids, the horse is still maintaining a round outline.

• The horse reacts to this and slows down.

• You can see how the horse's strides have become shorter.

• When the rider feels the horse has shortened enough he pushes him on, asking him to work from behind and make his stride longer.

LENGTHENING

Start by riding a 20-metre left circle in rising trot at the C end of the arena. Use the circle to help your horse take more of his weight on his hindquarters – use half-halts, as you would do when you shorten his stride. As you leave the 20-metre circle and ride into the CH corner, activate your horse's hindquarters but this time as you half-halt, instead of containing the energy in your hands, soften your hands so that they allow the energy forward and your horse can lengthen his stride. Count the number of lengthened strides from H to E and then go forwards to working trot and ride a circle at E. This allows you to re-balance your horse. Note: This exercise should be straightforward if your horse is balanced and supple and you prepare – remember that you are using the circle at E in working trot to re-balance him. Once you have re-established the balance, ride a few more lengthened strides from selected markers in the school. It is better to achieve a few good lengthened strides and then re-balance, than to try for too many lengthened strides and push your horse out of his rhythm.

TIP
Your horse will not automatically be able to produce superb lengthened strides – his ability to lengthen his stride can be built on as he becomes more balanced, strong and supple.

TIPS FOR LENGTHENING

- Use rising trot initially rather than trying to sit to produce lengthened strides. Rise a little higher out of the saddle to encourage your horse to move forward. When you want to return to working trot, decrease the size of your rises.

- Check that your horse is pushing off from both hindlegs. If you find that he goes wide behind, he has lost his balance. (When a horse goes wide behind he is trying to regain his balance by taking his hindlegs outside his forelegs.)

- If he just runs on faster rather than lengthening, or he goes into canter, bring your horse back to working trot immediately. Check that your aids are clear and that you are not bending him to the inside and asking him to canter.

- Once your horse can produce good lengthened strides along a long side and is moving straight, try riding this exercise across the diagonal.

- Before you ask for lengthened strides in sitting trot make sure your horse is established in producing them in rising trot. In sitting trot you must be able to absorb his movement and sit without driving down with your seat, otherwise any attempt to produce lengthened strides will result in him running instead.

- Remember that your horse's feet cannot hit the ground any further forward than his nose – as you create extra energy with your legs to produce lengthened strides, you must also allow with your hands so that he can stretch his head forward. He needs this freedom of head and neck to be able to stride out properly.

Turns

Turns and circles are a vital part of your horse's everyday schooling: they improve his suppleness and obedience, assist his balance and rhythm, and help to build up his muscles; they also enable you to introduce variation into his work. Riding turns and circles improves your own co-ordination of the aids.

Every turn, whether it's on to the centre line or across the diagonal, is actually a small part of a circle. Although you need to use all the aids – thought, weight, legs and hands – when riding a turn, it's worth undertaking the little exercise below to see how 'less is more' with many horses. All horses will respond to your weight aids although if they have been badly ridden for years they will be less sensitive and will need some re-education.

Using the weight aids

This exercise starts with you dismounted and sitting on a hard chair. Sit as if you are mounted on your horse – can you feel your seatbones? If you have trouble locating them, sit on your hands and rock your body back and forth – you should be able to feel your seatbones moving according to the angle of your pelvis. Keep your hands under your seatbones and adjust your upper body position so that you are in riding position. Now try advancing one hip slightly – can you feel that the seatbone on that side seems to roll forward a little? You may feel this better if you think of advancing your seatbone instead of your hip. Play around with this until you find what works for you. The next stage is to use this to turn your horse.

In the arena, on a loose rein, practise asking your horse to turn using your weight aids. Advance your left hip bone slightly if you wish to turn left and your right hip bone if you wish to go right. At the same time, use your outside leg to guide the horse around. Don't use your reins.

Your horse may not immediately understand your requests – although I've found that young horses just being backed certainly know what to do! As he becomes more familiar with you using your weight, so he will respond more. When a horse reacts sensitively to your weight aids, your leg and hand aids don't have to work so hard and the whole picture looks much more pleasant – as if you are doing virtually nothing when turning.

Circles

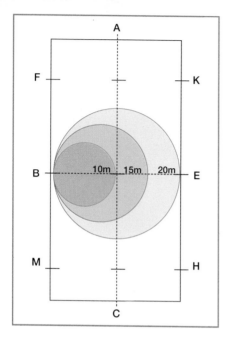

If you look at dressage tests, you'll see circles of various sizes incorporated into the sequences of movements, for example, 20-, 15- and 10-metre circles, as well as variations such as half a 20- or 10-metre circle, or two 10-metre circles joined together to create a figure of eight. Always start off riding larger circles as your horse will need a greater degree of balance and suppleness to cope with smaller circles.

▼ RIDING A 20-METRE CIRCLE

Twenty-metre circles can be ridden in three places in a 20 metre by 40 metre school – at either end (starting from A or C) and in the middle (starting from B or E). You can set yourself markers to help you ride the circle properly. If, as in the example here, you start at B on the right rein, your next marker will be on the centre line, halfway between X and A, then at E and then again on the centre line halfway between X and C before returning to your starting point of B.

● When starting a circle, leave the track directly after the marker – here the circle is starting at B – then ride a smooth curve to the next point.

● When rejoining the track, you should be back on the track just before the marker (E).

● This means that you are straight on the track as you pass the marker (E).

● You then move off the track just after the marker (E) to progress to the next one (centre line) on the circle.

● Circles should be continuous smooth curves so every step your horse takes is on a curve. Use your inside leg on the girth to keep the forward movement and to ask for the inside bend; use the inside rein to indicate the amount of bend needed. The outside rein prevents too much bend in the neck while the outside leg is ready, if required, to prevent the horse's quarters swinging out.

● Here (right) our rider is showing how the outside shoulder can be lost and then easily drifts off line.

BEND ▶

To execute a circle properly, a horse has to be balanced and straight – with uniform bend throughout his body from poll to tail, and with the hind feet following the same line as the fore feet. The smaller the circle, the more the horse has to bend, which is why you should ensure your horse can do large circles well before trying the more testing smaller circles.

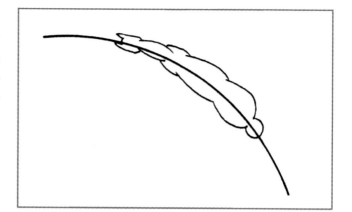

TROUBLESHOOTING

- If your horse has too much bend in his neck (right), his weight will be thrown onto his outside shoulder and you may well lose control of the shoulder so that the horse falls out of the circle. This is especially likely if your outside hand is weak and there is insufficient contact on the outside rein. Check your position and concentrate on staying upright in order to avoid unbalancing your horse. Use less inside rein and more outside rein. Riding exercises such as shoulder-fore (p.108) also helps.

- If your horse leans in on circles use more inside leg – in short, sharp bursts rather than with a prolonged pressure – and a more positive outside rein.

- Test whether your horse is ready to move on to smaller circles by gradually spiralling down from a 20-metre circle to a 15- or 10-metre circle. When you feel he has reached his limit, use your inside leg to ask him to move gradually back out onto the 20-metre circle again.

- If your horse's quarters fall out, use less inside rein and be more positive with your outside aids; your outside leg ceases to be passive and is used behind the girth to stop the quarters swinging out (left).

RIDING A 10-METRE CIRCLE ▶

To ride these smaller circles success-fully, your horse has to be much more balanced and supple than for a 20-metre circle. As the circle size decreases, so his inside hindleg has to work harder.

● On this 10-metre circle the horse's body is correctly bent and corresponding to the line he should be on.

● This horse is too straight and so his body is not following the line he should be travelling to achieve the correct bend.

● Here, you can see there is too much bend to the inside.

● Now, because the inside bend has been over-corrected, the horse is bent too much to the outside.

TIPS

- Ten-metre circles may be ridden at any of the markers in the school (right). When riding them at the corner markers, remember that the markers are 6 metres in from the short side of the school. Therefore, your circle will not quite touch the short side of the arena, but will be a metre out.

- To improve your accuracy use poles to mark out four 10-metre circles within one half of the 20 metre x 40 metre arena (below).

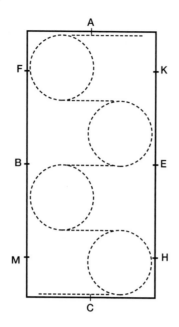

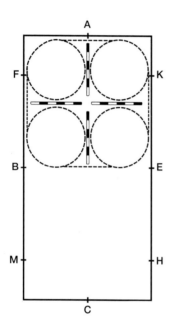

- If you can ride shoulder-in (p.110) you will have a better idea of controlling the bend, which will help you in riding smaller circles.

- In a dressage test you will be marked down if your circles are an irregular shape; if your horse is bending the wrong way; if the circle is the wrong size; or if your horse is on the forehand. Through practice you can avoid losing marks unnecessarily!

- Note how your horse performs and consider whether your riding could be affecting him: for example, is the persistent problem with his shoulder drifting out due to your position? Your horse's way of going will reveal whether you are sitting in balance or crookedly.

- Aim for a gradual, smooth and resistance-free change of bend as you move from one half circle to another.

- If your horse goes hollow or you feel him go unlevel in his steps you have probably asked too much of him in that the circle is too small for his degree of balance and engagement.

INCORPORATING CIRCLES INTO OTHER EXERCISES

There is endless scope for using circles in other exercises. Here are some ideas:

- Ride 10-metre circles in the loops of serpentines.

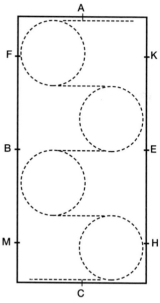

- Ride 20-metre circles and practise transitions. For example, do a walk to canter transition at four points in the 20-metre circle.

- Change the rein by riding two half 10-metre circles within a 20-metre circle.

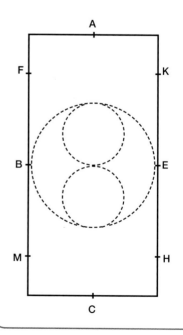

RIDING HALF CIRCLES ▶

There are a variety of ways in which to ride half circles. For instance, you can ride two half 20-metre circles, say from A to X and then X to C. Alternatively, you could ride two half 10-metre circles, such as from B to X and X to E. As you change from one half circle to another you need to change the bend and be straight for one stride. Photo 1 shows the rider coming off a right circle and approaching X. Photo 2 shows the horse over X as the rider prepares to change the bend to the left in order to ride from X to E.

Photo 3 shows the rider coming off the left hand circle and preparing to straighten the horse over X.

Another way to use half circles is to ride a half circle at a specific point, for example at M and then incline back to the track. Use several half circles, one after the other along the centre line, as a good exercise to help your horse's suppleness.

1

Loops and Serpentines

These are good exercises to help your horse's suppleness and they are suitable for including as part of your warm-up procedure. They are invaluable in helping you to understand how to use your weight aids and how to achieve the correct bend in your horse. Serpentines are basically straight lines and half circles joined together.

Riding serpentines (and loops) gives you the chance to practise changing the bend so your horse becomes much more flexible. If you are not familiar with these exercises, do them in walk first so that you can work out your aids: you have to be careful to co-ordinate the aids as each time the bend changes, the role of your hands changes: what was the inside hand becomes the outside hand and vice versa. Remember that the inside hand indicates the flexion, helped by the inside leg, which is also creating impulsion, while the outside hand controls the speed and the outside leg controls the horse's quarters. Ride a half-halt before each of the half circles in a serpentine and before you straighten up and prepare to change the bend.

Ride serpentines in walk and trot; don't attempt to canter them until your horse has learnt collection. He will also need to know how to do counter canter and a flying change. If you try to canter serpentines before he is ready, your horse will struggle with his balance and his confidence may also be dented – as indeed might yours!

▼ **SERPENTINES**

Serpentines also encourage the horse to soften to your inside leg and they assist you in learning the importance of looking ahead and planning a route. There is a lot for you to think about as you have to ensure that:

• each loop of the serpentine is the same width;

• each end of the loop has a well-shaped half circle;

• the horse is bent through the half circles and straight in between them;

• the rhythm and impulsion remains the same through the exercise.

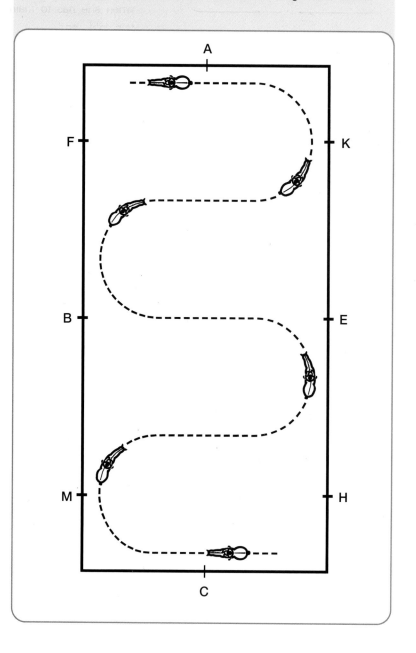

VARIATIONS ON A THEME

- Incorporate other elements into your serpentines. Examples include riding transitions (progressive and direct) at various points; halting on the centre line and then reining back; incorporating circles into the loops.

- Use half the width of the school to ride a serpentine – making a series of 10 metre half circles. Do this in walk or trot, not canter; if you trot, use sitting trot.

SERPENTINE TIPS

- Establish a good active trot before you start the exercise.

- Make use of half-halts as you move from one element of the exercise to another.

- Remember to change your diagonal as you cross the centre line if you are riding the serpentine in rising trot.

- Be aware of the bend and the shape of the half circle.

- To help you keep straight as you join one half circle to another, you can place poles to form a channel through which you ride.

- Don't forget your weight aids!

- Depending upon the school's size, you can ride three-, four- or five-loop serpentines. Remember that the more loops you include, the more demands will be made upon your horse's balance and engagement of the hindquarters.

- Use even numbers of loops in a serpentine if you want to change the rein as part of the exercise.

LOOPS ▶

- Shallow loops (usually 5m/15ft) can be ridden off the long side of the school or along the centre line. If the loop being ridden on the right rein along the K to H side of the arena, the rider has to think about bend at three points:

  - around the AK corner, when she has to maintain right bend.

  - as she comes off the track by K to ride the shallow loop, when she has to change the bend to the left.

  - as she prepares to return to the track at H, when she has to change to right bend again.

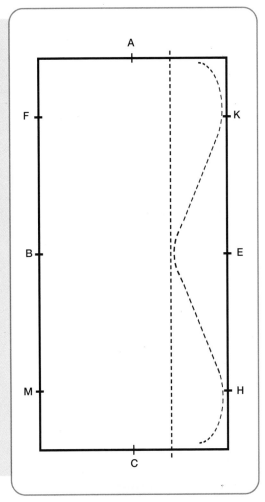

TIPS FOR LOOPS

- Use blocks or some kind of marker to indicate the route and to establish the width of the loop. In the above example, markers could be placed opposite K and H, a metre (3ft) or so off the track, and at E, 5m (15ft) off the track, so that the rider has some reference points.

- With both loops and serpentines, the changes of bend are gradual – think ahead and prepare so that the change of bend is a smooth process.

- Remember to use half-halts to gain your horse's attention and re-balance him before you ask for a change of bend.

- For variety, ride loops along the centre line.

- Loops can be used as a preparation for counter canter.

Lateral Work

When your horse is moving forwards with impulsion and is straight, it's time to think about getting him to understand your lateral aids – so he learns that pressure from your legs can mean move sideways as well as forwards.

Lateral work has many benefits. For instance, it will help your horse's balance and his acceptance of the bit as well as improve his obedience to your aids. In addition, regularly including lateral work in your horse's schooling programme will assist his physical development and be a useful tool to help overcome problems such as crookedness.

Turn on the forehand

Turn on the forehand and turn about the forehand will improve your horse's manoeuvrability and act as preparation for other lateral work. Apart from improving your horse's obedience to your leg aids and your co-ordination of the aids, turn on the forehand has a very practical application: it makes opening gates while out on hacks much easier!

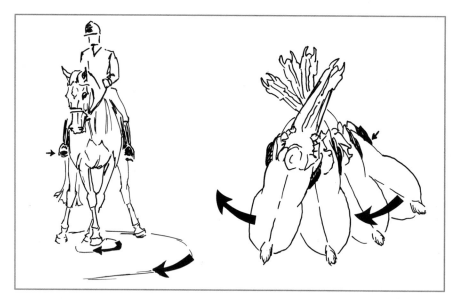

In turn on the forehand the horse changes direction by doing a 180-degree turn from halt – his forelegs march on the spot as his hindlegs describe a half circle around them.

Turn about the forehand is ridden from a slow walk. The movement is the same as turn on the forehand, except that the forelegs will move in a small semi-circle, rather then staying in more or less in the same place. The aids are the same (see below) and you do a half-halt to balance the horse before beginning the turn.

Riding a turn on the forehand

The sequence (right) shows a turn on the forehand to the right; the horse's head moves to the right and his hindlegs step around to the left. When your horse is learning the movement, it will be easier for him to flex his head away from the direction in which his quarters are moving, so in a right turn his head will be flexed to the right. Once he is proficient, the turn can be ridden with the flexion either way. If you are teaching your horse the movement ask him for one step, praise him as soon as he complies, then walk forward. Gradually build up the number of steps you ask him to take.

TURN ON THE FOREHAND ▶

- Ride your horse onto the inner track of your arena (about 1m/3ft in from the outside track) and halt. Aim for a square halt. With a horse that is learning the movement, halt facing the arena fence as this will effectively block forward movement.

- Your right rein maintains the flexion to the right while your left rein stops your horse walking forwards. You may need to half-halt on the left rein to stop your horse rushing through the movement.

- Use your right leg behind the girth to ask for your horse's hindquarters to move over: use repeated short aids to say 'over, over' rather than keeping the leg on. If you keep a constant pressure on with your leg aid your horse is likely to lean into it rather than move away. Timing your aids with the lifting of your horse's right hindleg will make the whole process much easier. Your horse should take slow deliberate steps.

- Keep your left leg on the girth to maintain impulsion and be ready to prevent the hindquarters swinging around too quickly.

- You should be able to feel your horse's right hindleg crossing over his left hindleg as he steps around.

- Once you have completed the turn, ride your horse forward in trot to get him thinking and moving forwards again.

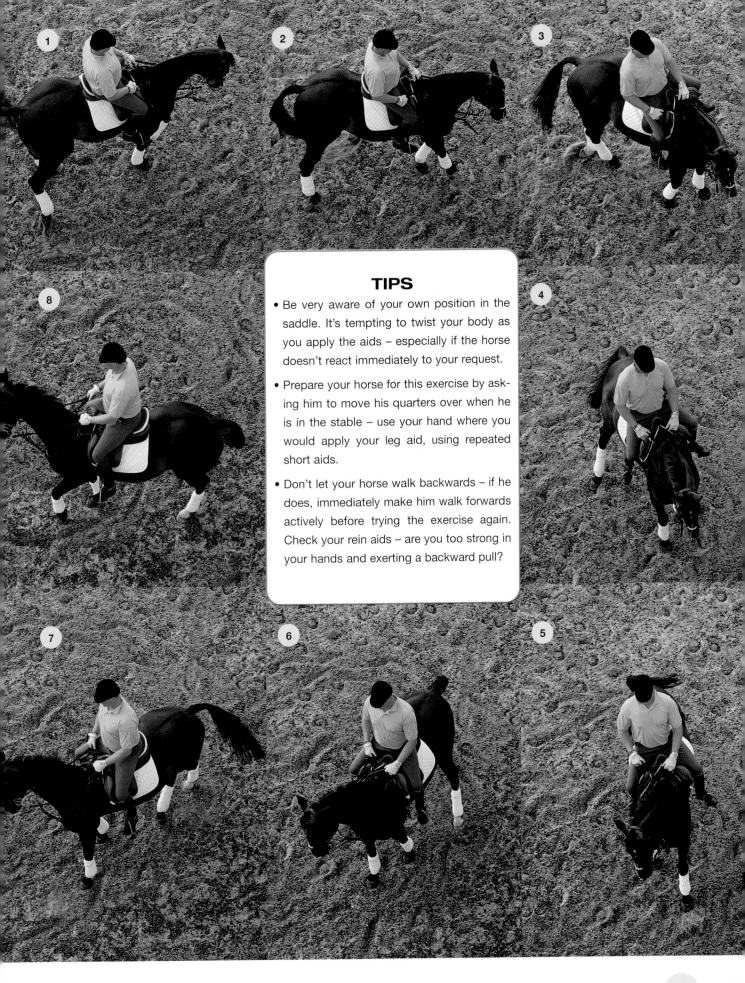

TIPS

- Be very aware of your own position in the saddle. It's tempting to twist your body as you apply the aids – especially if the horse doesn't react immediately to your request.

- Prepare your horse for this exercise by asking him to move his quarters over when he is in the stable – use your hand where you would apply your leg aid, using repeated short aids.

- Don't let your horse walk backwards – if he does, immediately make him walk forwards actively before trying the exercise again. Check your rein aids – are you too strong in your hands and exerting a backward pull?

Leg yielding

Leg yielding is often the first lateral work that horses and riders learn. As the name suggests, the horse yields to the rider's leg by moving away from it, crossing one fore- and one hindleg in front of the other fore- and hindleg as he moves diagonally forwards and sideways for a few steps. The horse has his body straight apart from a slight flexion away from the direction of travel. Therefore, if a horse is leg yielding to the left, he will be looking slightly right: the rider will just be able to see the corner of his right eye.

The exercise is taught in walk and is designed to encourage more response to the rider's leg aids, as well as improving the horse's suppleness and helping to produce a more rounder outline. When teaching leg yield, be happy with a couple of steps and then straighten and ride on.

The exercise can be ridden on circles or from straight lines, for example moving from the centre or quarter line to the outside track. Spiralling in and out of a circle involves leg yielding and some horses find this much easier.

▼ RIDING LEG YIELD TO THE LEFT

- Use your right hand to ask for slight flexion of your horse's head to the right. Your left hand prevents excessive bend and monitors the speed. You may need to half-halt on the left rein to keep control of the shoulder, especially if your horse tries to run through the movement.

- Use your right leg to ask for sideways movement and your left leg to maintain the forward movement and keep your horse from falling too much to the left as shown in photo 4. Photo 5 shows an incorrect position resulting in stiffening through the forehand and tilting of the head.

Shoulder-fore and shoulder-in

Both shoulder-fore and shoulder-in require the horse's forehand to be off the track but to varying degrees. With shoulder-fore the forehand is just off the track, with shoulder-in the forehand should be at an angle of about 30 degrees to the side of the arena. Shoulder-fore is an introduction to shoulder-in but is also useful for various other work – for example, to straighten a horse by bringing the shoulders in line with the hindquarters rather than pushing the hindquarters out. Shoulder-in is an invaluable exercise for straightening the horse and increasing his suppleness and engagement.

In shoulder-in the horse's inside foreleg passes and crosses over the outside foreleg. The inside hindleg steps well under as it lifts and propels the horse forwards, but the hindlegs do not cross. This is a three-track movement with the outside hindleg making one track, the outside fore and inside hind being on the same line and making the second track, and the inside foreleg making the third track.

However, if riding a narrower TB type of horse it must be taken into consideration that three-track is very little angle and it is permissible to ride four tracks which would take narrower horses onto the correct angle.

◀ SHOULDER-FORE

In shoulder-fore use your inside rein to create bend and your outside rein to bring the shoulders off the track. Your inside leg asks for the sideways movement and your outside hand also controls the speed. Once your horse can continue in shoulder-fore along the length of the school easily on both reins, you can progress to shoulder-in.

▶ Do this by asking for more bend and increasing the angle until the full 30-degree three-track movement of shoulder-in is achieved.

Teaching shoulder-in

There are several approaches to teaching a horse shoulder-in, other than simply developing the movement from shoulder-fore (p.108). Many trainers ride a 10-metre circle in the corner of the school and then maintain the bend out of the circle, holding the horse in shoulder-in position as they carry on along the track.

Shoulder-in can also be ridden on a large circle, asking for a couple of steps initially, then straightening the horse and riding him forwards. The horse should always be moving forwards and sideways freely, without any tension in his body.

• The horse is bent around the rider's inside leg and the near hind is coming well under the body.

• The near hind and off fore are on the ground, making the second of the three tracks of this movement.

▼ RIDING SHOULDER-IN

- In shoulder-in your horse's outside shoulder leads, so your own shoulders need to be turned slightly to the inside. By advancing your outside hip bone slightly so that it points along the line you plan to ride, you position your shoulders correctly, and by almost imperceptibly following the movement of your horse's back with your hips, you allow him to move underneath you.

- Raising your inside hand slightly can assist in flexing the horse to the inside.

- Maintaining your inside leg position will encourage your horse to bend around your inside leg.

- Your inside leg only comes into play if the horse starts to fall to the insider or becomes inactive.

- The outside leg maintains its position slightly behind the girth where it acts as a passive barrier only to be activated if you feel your horse's quarters swinging out.

- Now the near fore and off hind are activated, on two different tracks…

…and the near fore comes across. This horse takes quite large swinging steps – he needs to have plenty of mobility in his hindquarters and shoulders to do this.

Turn on the haunches

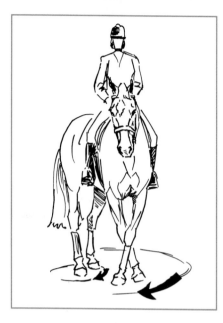

Turns on the haunches, known as pirouettes when ridden in a dressage test, are more difficult than turns on the forehand (p.104). In a turn on the haunches, the horse has to turn in a circle, or part of a circle, by moving his forehand around his hindquarters. The sequence of footfalls is the same as in walk, with the horse ideally keeping the same tempo, so his steps do not slow down. He will lift and return his inside hind foot to the same place each time and there will be a slight bend through his body in the direction his shoulders are moving.

To perform this movement well you need to be able to collect your horse's walk and your horse has to be able to carry more of his weight on his quarters. However, you can begin to teach this movement by riding a turn on the haunches on a larger circle so that your horse moves his forehand around his quarters but also walks a circle with his hindlegs.

1

2

3

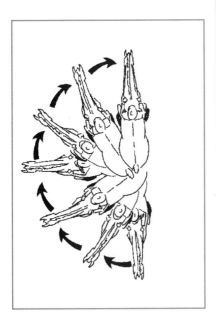

TIPS

• When riding the half-halt, remember your leg aid – in this exercise you would remove the energy from the steps if you half-halted just by using the outside rein. You need to use your legs as well, especially the inside one, which is maintaining the activity in your horse's inside hind.

• Keep your horse in a rounded outline throughout the turn. If he tenses up and hollows against your hand, walk forward and go back to just asking for one step before gradually building up to a full turn again.

• Keep the rhythm of your horse's walk in your mind – if you feel he is losing rhythm, go back to riding the turn on a larger circle. Also do this if he starts to pivot rather than moving his hindlegs up and down.

• Get creative! There are lots of shapes you can ride in the school using quarter or full turns on the haunches. However, do not ride too many turns in quick succession, as they are hard work for the horse.

• These turns help to collect your horse so use them before other exercises. For example, make a turn on the haunches before asking for a transition to trot or canter.

continued overleaf

Polework

Poles can be used in a wide variety of ways to help your horse's rhythm, balance, co-ordination and concentration. Polework benefits flatwork and jumping, as the horse is encouraged to pick up his feet and use his hindquarters and shoulders productively. Poles are useful in regulating a horse's paces and adding interest to his work. They can also be used to address specific problems such as lack of dexterity and difficulty in achieving correct canter strike-offs.

A box of poles

Working with a box of poles improves the dexterity and co-ordination of both horse and rider. The repetition and discipline also helps to relax excitable horses. With all of these exercises do not overdo the number of repetitions – horses learn surprisingly quickly and will become bored if asked to repeat exercises over and again. If your horse makes a good job of something at the first attempt then move on and change something rather than bore him.

Create a box of poles, preferably using 4m (12ft) poles rather than 3m (10ft) poles. Use the box in any of the ways below, ensuring that you do the exercises on both reins so that each side of the horse is worked.

USING THE GRID ▶

- Walk in over one pole and out over the opposite pole.

- Walk in over one pole, making a gradual turn to ride out over an adjacent pole.

- Walk in and ride a loop, walking out over the same pole.

- Walk in and out, turning left or right, riding into the box again over a different pole. Work around the box until you reach your starting point.

- Ride a small circle within the box (your horse needs to be supple in order to do this).

CO-ORDINATION EXERCISE ▶

This exercise, which involves riding across the corners of the box, helps your co-ordination of the aids and ensures that you use both inside and outside aids to achieve your aim. As you ride into the box, use your outside leg to push your horse over. While the inside rein asks for flexion, the outside rein controls the speed; the inside leg maintains the impulsion. Reverse the aids as you ride out of the box, so that your inside leg becomes your outside leg and pushes the horse over; the other aids are also reversed.

▲ A ROW OF POLES

- Poles arranged in a row along the side of the school can be used at walk, trot and canter. They improve a horse's rhythm, balance and co-ordination – having the same effect on the rider. Always use an odd number of poles and adjust the distance between them to suit your horse. For example, for trot poles start by placing them 1.4m (4½ft) apart for a 16hh horse – ideally he should place his feet in the middle of the distance between each pole. Discipline yourself to ride through the centre of the poles, keeping the rhythm consistent throughout.

- As a variation on this exercise, set the poles out on the centre line and ride down them at an angle to lengthen the trot. For example, ride from right to left, starting at the far right of the first pole and aiming at the far left of the last pole.

- You can set poles further apart (2.7m/9ft), and then ride circles over them, gradually working your way through a line of poles. The circling helps to engage the horse's hindlegs. As you ride over the last pole, try to keep the same energy that you created over the poles in your flatwork.

TIPS

- Don't use just two poles in a line as your horse may try to jump both rather than trotting over them.

- Adjust distances gradually, a couple of centimetres/inch or so at a time, in order to find the best distance for your horse.

- If your horse rushes on the approach to a row of poles, use half-halts to steady and re-balance him. Alternatively, turn him away onto a circle and steady the pace, extending the circle to take in the poles when he is calmer. Do this exercise in trot: the circles will help to shorten him and engage his hindlegs, while going over the poles will elevate his stride a little. The combined effect should be a more energetic trot, in a more compact frame – try to keep this feeling of extra energy and more lift to the trot when you leave the poles.

- As you go over the poles remember to release your hand a little, opening your fingers around the rein, so that your horse has a little more freedom in his head and neck, but don't throw away the contact.

Semi-circle of poles

Use poles in a semi-circle on a corner or elsewhere in the school to give another dimension to your polework. Initially, work over the centre of the poles, remembering to keep the bend to the inside and using the outside aids to keep your horse on the correct line. Then ride a little wider, going over the outside edge of the poles, keeping the rhythm and balance consistent.

Raised poles

Once your horse is working confidently over poles on the ground, raise alternate ends of the poles. This encourages him to flex his joints more and you should feel him really lifting his body underneath you. It is important to keep him in a steady trot rhythm.

TIPS

- Have someone on the ground to adjust the poles for you. This enables you to keep the session flowing.

- Inexperienced horses may initially stumble when trying to negotiate poles. Check the distances. Don't get too flustered and don't try to help the horse too much – he has to learn to sort his feet out.

- Raising both ends of the poles is hard work for the horse, so if you do this be careful not to overdo the exercises.

Jumping

Jumping should be included in every horse's training. Apart from the fact that you might discover your horse has a real talent for it, jumping adds variety to his work and, if you use gymnastic jumping exercises, makes him more supple, balanced and co-ordinated.

It is important to be aware of the horse and rider's confidence when jumping. Both can soon lose confidence if they are over-faced at a fence. However, there is no need to jump large fences – grids built of small obstacles can be testing and will also help to develop the horse's musculature.

Fences and grids

As we've already seen, working over poles helps a horse to use himself more efficiently and gives a boost to his paces. The next step after poles is to start introducing fences, for instance a placing pole to a small crossed pole (see diagram). Crossed poles guide the horse to the centre of the fence – the principles of going forward and straight apply just as much over fences as they do on the flat. The important point to remember is to ensure the horse keeps straight after the fence. Once he is more experienced, you can ask him to start jumping fences at angles and make turns after fences, but initially he must learn that he goes forward and straight.

Provide your horse with a variety of fences – crossed poles, uprights, spreads and parallels. When he is jumping single fences happily you can start to introduce combinations. These can vary from a double to a treble, to a whole line of fences, known as a grid, where the horse may be jumping, say, five fences, one after the other. Gridwork is beneficial for both horse and rider and can also be used for a whole host of problems, such as horses that rush, those that use themselves inefficiently or make a poor shape over a fence, horses that are careless, those that refuse and those that take their own line instead of listening to the rider. Grids can also be used to sharpen up a rider's reactions, teach horse and rider how to take strides out to improve their chances of winning in a jump-off, improve a rider's steering and generally increase confidence in both horse and rider.

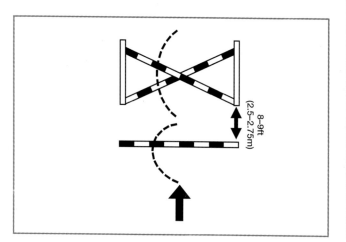

• This pair jumped the first upright in good balance, so they have no trouble in making one level stride between the two elements. If the horse had been backing off the first fence, he might have landed short which would have resulted in the rider having to push on to make the distance (this is where the lengthening and shortening of stride exercises on the flat are of help).

▼ SIMPLE GRID

This exercise involves two upright fences, with a non-jumping stride in between, and then two non-jumping strides to a parallel fence. How well you jump into a grid will determine how well your horse jumps out! In this case, the out fence will need more pace on the approach than the in fence.

FINDING YOUR JUMPING POSITION

Practise your jumping skills dismounted! Stand on a jump pole and adopt the jumping position – you may need to make minor adjustments until you find your balance. Once you have found it, experiment a little – tip forward just a tad and you'll see how easy it is for you to lose it. Get used to the feel of balancing in your jumping position and, once back on board your horse, remember how vital your position was to your balance. Try to keep this independent balanced seat when riding.

● The horse makes another good job over the second upright so he is able to fit in two level strides before taking off for the final element.

● As a result, he makes nothing of the parallel fence. Jumping with this much confidence is the result of good, progressive work, building the horse's skills, trust and confidence.

GRID FOR A CARELESS OR IMPULSIVE HORSE

Despite your best efforts, some horses insist on rushing, with the inevitable result that fences will be knocked down. This grid brings the horse in off a shorter approach that also involves negotiating poles – this keeps his brain and body occupied and reduces the chance of him zooming off on approach to the fences themselves. The two fences at either end of the grid are fairly acute crossed poles; there is a single crossed pole in the middle and placing poles in between each fence. The acute crosses are intended to make the horse pick up his front and back legs while the ground poles discourage rushing and encourage round, even strides in between the fences. When you land after the last fence you can choose to go in either direction, but still on a curve, and with ground poles, to make your horse back off and lessen the chance of him running off. You will probably need to use this grid on several occasions to ensure he gets the message.

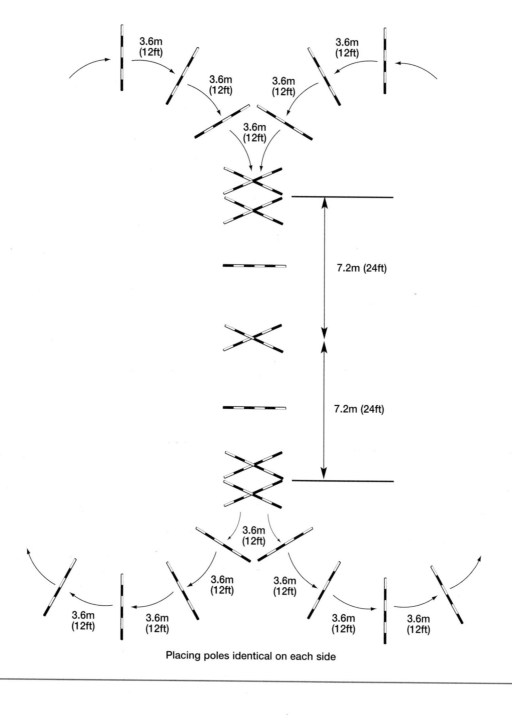

Placing poles identical on each side

TIPS FOR BUILDING AND NEGOTIATING GRIDS

• Jumping grids can be daunting to some horses – they may start to back off when they see the mass of poles and fillers in front of them. Build your horse's exposure to fences gradually, introducing him to all the sights he is likely to see. Even if he shows great talent, don't be tempted to skip any basic work because all horses hit problems at some point and it will be much harder to address them if your foundation work is shaky.

• When you are building combinations you are aiming for your horse to make a good rounded jump over each fence. You must therefore pay careful attention to the distances:

For a 15.2hh–16.2hh horse the average stride length is 3.6m (12ft). Learn to pace out a distance of 90cm (3ft) so you can pace the distance between each fence. When pacing, remember to allow for the landing and take-off points – allow 1.8m (6ft) for each. Therefore the distance between two fences with one non-jumping stride in between will be a total of 7.2m (24ft) – 1.8m (6ft) to allow for landing, 3.6m (12ft) for the stride and 1.8m (6ft) to allow for take off.

When the fences are under 90cm (3ft) shorten the distance between them, otherwise the horse may struggle to make the distance. For example, a double with one non-jumping stride will have 7.2m (24ft) between the two elements; however, if the elements are small, say 60cm (2ft), reduce the distance in between by about 90cm (3ft) to 6.3m (21ft). Note how your horse copes and adjust the distance again if necessary.

• When building combinations for novice horses make the first fence particularly inviting, such as an ascending oxer.

• Poles used as ground lines (to encourage your horse to lower his head and neck on approach to the fence) should always be used in front of the fence, not behind it. Fillers should also be put underneath front rails and not behind them.

Bounce fences

Bounce fences don't have a non-jumping stride in between them: the horse's front feet land but then have to pick up immediately to take off for the second fence just as his hind feet touch the ground. These fences, therefore, need more athleticism and power from the horse, as well as requiring him to think quickly. Once your horse is comfortable with jumping fences in a grid, you can introduce a bounce fence. Initially, this must be small so your horse has the chance to realise what he has to do – start off with one small crosspole fence to a small vertical. You could then add another fence so he is making two bounce jumps. Don't make a bounce grid consist of more than five fences, as the effort involved on the horse's part is strenuous, particularly as the fences get higher.

WHY BOUNCE?

Bounce fences teach a horse to be sharper in his shoulders and to use his hindlegs more actively: horses who have had this training will find obstacles on cross country courses, such as drops and steps, much easier.

A BOUNCE BOX

1 An alternative way of using a bounce is to build a box of fences in the middle of the arena so that you can ride a figure of eight, taking in the bounces as you go.

2 & 3 The horse here is experienced so the fences are reasonably large. At first, the fences should be no more than 90cm (3ft) high, as the gymnastic ability needed to negotiate bounces at this height is tremendous. The distance between bounce fences should not be less than 3.6m (12ft), unless they are very small.

4 & 5 Here you can see that the rider is thinking ahead – as she lands after the first set of fences she is preparing for a right turn. She keeps the momentum as she approaches the second set of fences.

6 & 7 On the approach she sits up and looks ahead – bounces are great for improving rider balance and suppleness.

8 & 9 With bounce fences, just as with other types of obstacle, it is important to keep the horse on line, in balance and with plenty of impulsion. Using a bounce box gives you the challenge of keeping the more active bouncy stride all the way through the exercise. Successful completion of the exercise – hard work but an invaluable lesson.

ADAPTING A BOX GRID

• A box of fences can be adapted so that there are one or two non-jumping strides between obstacles. By then laying ground poles so that the jumps can be approached from either direction, you make a versatile grid that can be approached off either rein. This box grid consisting of fences A, B, C and D can be jumped from either rein. More options have then been added by the inclusion of jumps E and F. Now the rider can, for instance, jump in over D and out over E or in over A and out over E or F, or in over F and out over C, or in over E and out over D or A. Having this many options is especially useful if the horse tends to make his own decisions: because the rider can change the route all the time he learns not to anticipate but to wait for instructions from the rider.

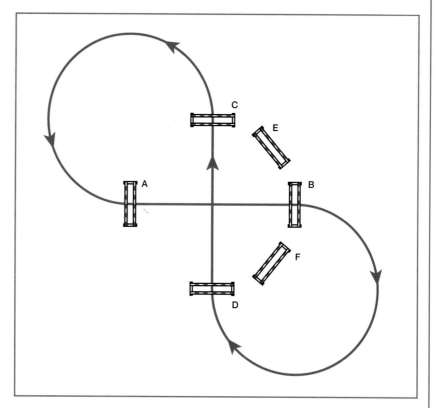

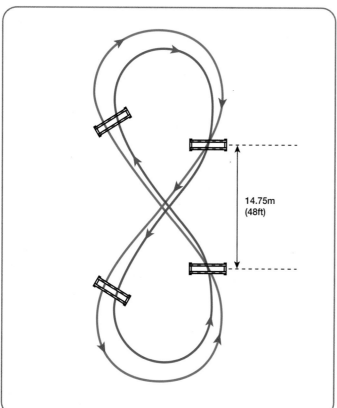

14.75m
(48ft)

• This variation on the box grid shows how to ride a figure of eight and reduce the number of strides taken to do so. First ride the fences allowing plenty of room for turns and counting the number of strides it takes to complete the figure of eight. Then ride the same route but making tighter turns and see how much difference this makes to the overall number of strides. This is good practice for jump-off techniques: if your horse can jump cleanly and take a shorter route, there is no need to risk knocking down a fence by riding too fast.

TIPS FOR SUCCESSFUL JUMPING LESSONS

- Always warm up thoroughly before a jumping session, as your horse will be using many muscles. Cooling down properly is also important.

- Don't be tempted to keep going for too long when your horse is jumping well. As he becomes tired, his performance will deteriorate: finish on a good note.

- If you work through grids and your horse loses confidence, go back a step, lower the fences or use an easier exercise to regain his trust.

- Make sure you school over different combinations, such as upright to a spread, upright to a parallel and so on.

- Gridwork is a great gymnastic exercise for both horse and rider but you must also learn to jump courses. Include both elements in your schooling programme.

- A balanced canter is the key to good jumping: practise canter exercises on the flat, such as lengthening and shortening the stride, direct transitions to and from canter, and riding loops and circles. These will all help to improve your horse's suppleness, engagement and balance, and will be invaluable for your jumping sessions.

Jumping on a circle

This exercise involves constructing two small fences on a 20-metre circle (for example at B and E) so that the rider can pop over them without disturbing the rhythm of the trot or canter.

To start with, simply place a pole at B and E and trot your horse around on a 20-metre circle. You need to keep the rhythm in your rising trot and resist the temptation to start fiddling with the reins as you approach the poles. When your horse has got the idea, you can then replace the poles with jumps. The idea is to keep coming around, letting him sort out his own feet – all you have to concentrate on is riding a good circle in rhythm. Remember to do this exercise equally on both reins because the inside hind leg is doing more work than the outside leg.

When you and your horse are happy in trot, you can move up a gear into canter. Remember to concentrate on the rhythm, keeping your horse in a balanced frame and just coming on round to the fences without trying to place him or look for a stride.

KEEPING A RHYTHM

This exercise helps you learn about rhythm. It will help to slow a horse that is naturally onward-bound, and is also useful if you tend to 'rush' at fences – do you fling yourself forward well before the fence? Or try to push your horse out of his natural rhythm? A tendency to rush may be due to anxiety about the fences – by keeping them small and giving yourself plenty to think about, you should soon find yourself getting on with the job rather than worrying!

TWO FENCES ON A CIRCLE ▶

1 & 2 Over this small spread, the rider is already looking to the right, preparing her line.

3 The partnership keeps the same rhythm on the circle and through the approach, landing and get away from the fence.

4 During this exercise, the rider still has to think about riding a good circle and ensuring that her horse does not go off line by swinging his quarters in or out.

5 & 6 This exercise also teaches the rider to wait for the fence so that the horse can negotiate it calmly without disturbing his rhythm and balance.

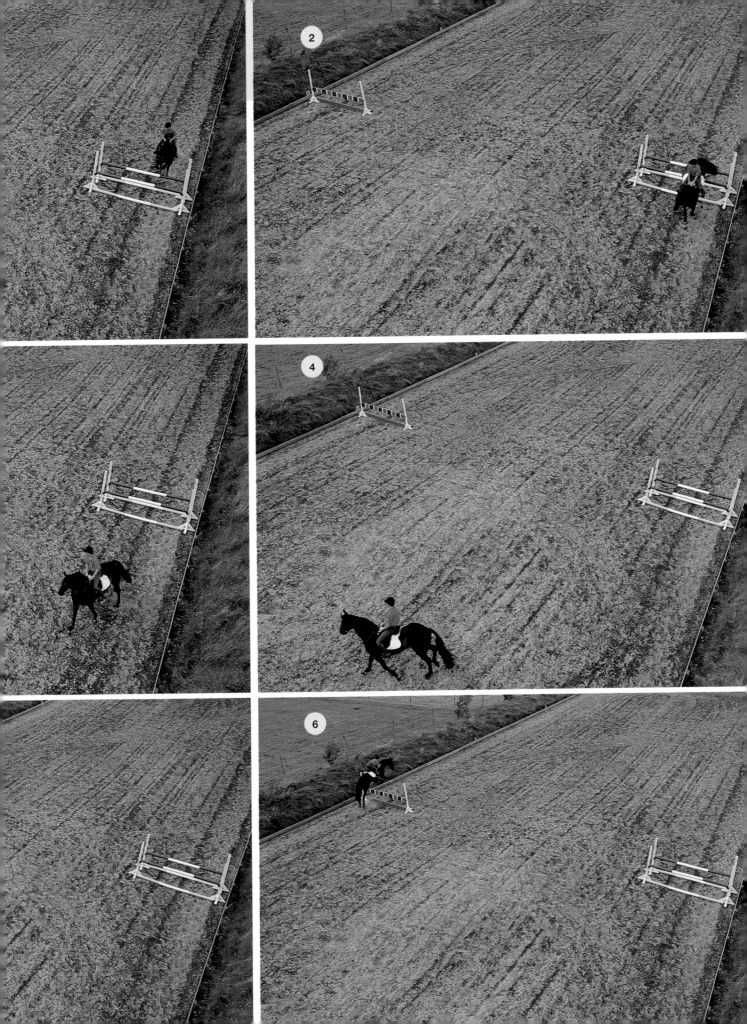

Riding courses

The objective of the gymnastic jumping exercises is to improve the horse's agility and confidence, build his muscles and teach him how to use himself effectively and efficiently. There will also be an improvement in co-ordination and balance. The rider benefits, too, becoming sharper in their thinking and reactions, more agile and more confident. However, all these exercises have the same ultimate aim: to produce a horse and rider capable of jumping clear over a showjumping course.

Techniques for riding a course

This next exercise uses four fences but is ideal for practising the art of riding courses. Erect two fences along one long side of the school – the distance between them can be varied from one or two strides to a longer distance (such as four or five strides). What you do will depend on how much room you have.

Then erect another two fences, each at an angle to the uprights already placed along the arena fence line.

RIDING THE COURSE ▶

1 The rider has started the exercise on the left rein and is negotiating the first upright.

2 As she approaches and jumps the second fence, she needs to keep straight but must also be thinking of the turn ahead.

3 Once over, she can use as little or as much of the arena as she needs to come across the diagonal to the parallel. With a long run in to a fence, it's easy for both horse and rider to lose focus and for the horse to lose impulsion. The rider must be aware of this and keep riding positively forwards.

4 As she approaches the parallel, she must remember that there is a right-hand turn after it, which she needs to pre-pare for in advance, opening the right rein a little and using the outside aids so that she can ride a smooth turn.

5 Again there is a long diagonal where the rider has to be wary of letting her horse fall on to his forehand. She must retain the rhythm and impulsion so will probably use half-halts to re-balance her horse, activate his hindquarters and ensure that he is paying attention.

Practising 'dog legs'

Many courses include fences that are on related distances: there may be several strides between the fences but how you jump one fence affects how you jump the next. However, these fences may not be on a straight line so you should practise jumping sequences that involve sharp turns. This exercise can be ridden from either direction and can also incorporate the fences alongside the arena edge. The rider has to have good control and be thinking ahead while the horse has to be supple and balanced. It's important that horse and rider flow on through this exercise.

◀ Here the pair jump the upright from a straight approach.

▼ The rider continues to go straight after the fence for a stride or so...
...then she has to ride more of a curved line so that she can get her approach correct for the next fence.

◀ This curve enables her to ride straight down to the parallel...
...where the pair successfully pop over.

TIPS

- As your horse becomes more confident and obedient with his jumping, you can add interest by taking fences at an angle. This skill is useful for jump offs as it enables you to take more direct lines between fences and reduce the overall number of strides, thus saving valuable time.

- Remember that your horse will go where you look, so you must look ahead. Here, you can see the rider looking up. Note also that her body position is nice and level.

- Teach yourself to ride better turns into fences by placing poles and cones at strategic points. The poles around the corner act as a guide to help you ride a balanced corner and then straight approach to the fence. If you want to practise riding into a fence with a sharper turn and a shorter approach, use a marker to guide you, such as the cone shown below.

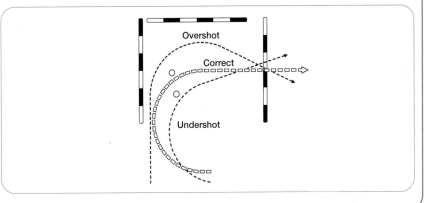

Western Riding

Riding Western is something that every rider should try so that they can feel just how light and responsive a horse can be. The training that Western horses and riders receive is of benefit to any horse and rider partnership, irrespective of their equestrian discipline. Western horses are ridden on a light contact and in relatively long outlines compared to dressage horses yet they can execute amazing movements with ease and without resistance. They are also relaxed and calm in all kinds of situations. So put aside any misconceptions you might have of Western riding – forget everything you've seen in the cowboy movies – and prepare to enter a world where lightness, harmony and a horse that is a real pleasure to ride are key factors.

BOB MAYHEW

A respected Western rider and trainer, Bob Mayhew has a Quarter Horse stud in the UK and was one of the first Europeans to become a judge of reining (a specialist Western riding sport) in the USA.

The paces

Western riding concerns itself with three of the horse's four paces: walk, trot (jog) and canter (lope). The gallop is rarely used, apart from when a horse goes from a gallop to a sliding stop.

WALK ▶

As he walks, a horse moves each of his legs individually in a four-time sequence: both of his legs on one side and then both legs on the other side. This means that he has to constantly re-adjust his balance – the rider therefore needs to help him as much as possible by being in a balanced position. If an imaginary line were to be drawn from the Western rider's ear downwards, it should go through the shoulder, the hip and the back of the heel, just as it should for a dressage rider. The difference between the two riders is in how they apply the aids, as we shall see later. Western riders look for a flat, ground-covering walk from their horses.

JOG ▶

This is basically a slow trot, moving from one diagonal pair of legs to the other. Compared to dressage riders, Western riders want less knee and hock action from their horses, and a shorter stride. The horse is expected to carry himself with a more or less level topline. This is only a four-year-old horse, just three months into her training programme, but she already shows the relaxed, calm attitude and soft stride that Western riders seek.

LOPE ▶

Lope is a slow canter in a rolling three-beat rhythm, with each stride being shorter and slower than a dressage-style canter. As a result the horse spends more time on one leg and the rocking motion of the pace is increased.

Above: The horse is loping to the right and is just finishing a sequence of footfalls as the leading leg, the off fore, comes to the ground.

Left: The rolling motion, so characteristic of the Western horse's lope, results from a slight break in the sequence of footfalls. The sequence is not an even 1, 2, 3 beats, instead there is a slight hesitation after the first stride so it is more of a 1, 2-3 rhythm. The break between the first beat and the second and third beats is because of the time taken in the rolling motion – in the sequence shown you can see how the horse's back lifts. The rider has to learn to absorb this lift through their lower back.

Below: In the third beat of the sequence, the horse is about to take the weight onto her leading leg. Look at the level of her head compared to the previous two photographs and the level of the quarters. You can see the rise and fall of her body, which is what produces the rolling sensation.

Western training principles

THE BEST HORSE FOR THE JOB?

American quarter horses are the choice of many Western riders, and as they are fairly mature by two years old, it's possible that they may even be backed at this age and then turned away. However, the age at which a horse is first ridden will depend upon the individual's maturity.

A good Western riding horse:

- stays calm and relaxed;
- doesn't challenge the rider's control;

- is a soft, supple, responsive ride;
- moves away from leg pressure;
- stops on command;
- stands square.

Western-trained horses are equipped to deal with the many situations they may expect to meet in their working environment. These can include cutting cattle, negotiating steep ascents or descents, dragging logs behind them, fording rivers or moving carefully along narrow, boulder-strewn tracks. Even though many Western horses are now solely pleasure animals, their training still equips them with the skills to deal calmly with life.

The horse's training programme includes exercises that help him become soft and supple, teach him to be responsive, to 'give his face' and to move his hips around – all aimed towards the rider having total control over his horse's body, both front and back end.

Starting young

The training of a Western riding horse starts early. From foalhood they are well-handled and they learn about being led, moving away from pressure on the ground (such as moving their quarters or shoulders over and backing up), standing in their own space and walking over obstacles on the ground.

Rewarding every try

Western trainers often speak of 'rewarding the horse's every try' so the horse, being an animal that genuinely wants to please anyway, becomes even more keen to do as he's asked. By looking for little tries and rewarding these efforts, trainers believe they produce a willing equine partner that enjoys his work. Throughout, the emphasis is on keeping the horse happy and relaxed – otherwise he cannot learn. Training sessions are kept short but regular.

Making it easy

The underlying principle of the training is to make it easy for the horse to do what you want him to do and make it difficult for him to disobey. This means that the trainer has to prepare the lesson and set up the situation so that the easiest option for the horse is to do as he is asked. Horses like an easy life, and as long as you are asking them a reasonable question, they will comply with the right answer: if you ask a horse to do something that he is neither physically nor mentally capable of doing, then your question is not reasonable. Nor is it right to expect a horse to do something if you have not clearly explained what it is you want of him.

STARTING IN WALK

Walk is a great training pace. It enables both horse and rider to have the time to fully understand what they are doing. Once a horse has learnt his lessons well in walk, he will progress to jog. The lessons will be consolidated there before he moves on to learning how to do the exercise in lope.

▼ 'GIVING FACE'

When the horse 'gives his face' he yields to the slightest pressure, dropping his head down or moving his head to either side. There is no resistance in his jaw or neck and he willingly does as he is asked. Before a Western rider even thinks of moving off from halt, he expects his horse to flex at the poll. Suppleness is the key to this – the horse would also be expected to flex his head and neck sideways without moving his shoulders.

During his training a young Western horse will be worked loose in a round pen so that he learns to balance himself at all gaits and ensuring he doesn't 'motorbike' around corners. As part of his training and to teach him to give to pressure on the bit, the reins are individually tied to the saddle so that in effect his head is tied to one side. The rein is not tight as there has to be enough room for him to escape the pressure. If he resists the pressure, he is pulling against himself. He will quickly learn to flex to one side and be comfortable. Both reins are also tied to the stirrups: if he flexes at the poll, the stirrups hang naturally and there is no pressure on his mouth. If, however, he raises his head then the stirrups, via the reins, will apply pressure. The important point with these exercises is that the trainer must know where the horse should carry his head in order to adjust the rein length accordingly. Horses want to be comfortable so they quickly learn how to escape pressure.

• **Above:** You can here see how light the rein contact is. The horse gives easily to the bridle. Once this 'giving of the face' has been achieved, the Western rider would ask the horse to move forward.

• **Right:** The rein pressure is very light but as you can see the horse yields to this light touch and shows how flexible he is. The reward for his compliance is a relaxation of the rein pressure – if this is not done then the horse learns to lean on the bit.

The aids

As a Western rider, you are ultimately aiming to be able to influence your horse's pace without driving him with your legs. While remaining upright and relaxed in the saddle, you allow your pelvis to move with your horse; you can then affect his speed by increasing or decreasing the pace or length of your pelvic movement.

Weight aids

You aim to tell your horse what you want him to do through body position and the use of weight. Weight aids are given by stepping into one stirrup (placing more weight in one stirrup than the other). By doing this you encourage your horse to move to the same side, seeking out your weight. Western riders do not lean to the side with their shoulders when they use their weight this way, it is much more of a subtle weight transference on to one seatbone.

For instance, to stop your horse you sit down in the saddle, taking the weight down into your heels so your legs are forward. You would also 'take the life' out of your body. If you want your horse to back up, you step into your stirrups more, putting more weight into your heels and sitting slightly back in the saddle. Take the slack out of the reins but do not pull to make your horse step back.

To ask a horse to go forward you incline your body forward very slightly and take some of the weight out of your heels.

• The objective is for your horse to respond to the lightest of aids.

USING THE REINS

The reins are used as an enhancement of the leg and weight aids. Aim to use them softly, applying the aids carefully so that you can feel immediately a horse gives to the rein. A Western rider uses the reins in five different ways:

NECK REIN: the rein is laid against the horse's neck and he moves away from it.

LEADING REIN: the rein is taken out to one side and the horse follows.

STOP OR REIN BACK: both reins are drawn back to make a horse stop or rein back or to encourage collection.

MOVING THE SHOULDER: one rein is held up and forward in front of the saddle horn to move the horse's shoulder away from the rein.

MOVING THE HIP: one rein is taken towards the rider's hip to help the horse move his hip in the opposite direction.

Control of the horse's body

Several elements of Western training assist the rider in achieving the goal of having total control over the horse's body. Of these, direct bend, indirect bend and hip displacement exercises are all important. Once his horses understand the exercises separately Bob Mayhew combines them into the 'snake trail', a zig-zag movement that is good preparation for other advanced moves.

▲ DIRECT BEND

The horse is looking in the direction he is going and is asked to step out with his inside front foot – this is good preparation for later exercises, such as a 360-degree spin. The rider uses the inside rein to ask the horse to 'give his face' and flex softly to the inside. The outside rein is against the horse's neck (this will ultimately help the horse to understand and respond to a neck rein aid).

Then the rider steps on the inside stirrup and moves his inside leg away while his outside leg pushes the horse over.

When the horse takes a step to the inside, he is rewarded by being 'turned loose' – the inside rein asking for the flexion is released. The horse is then walked forward for a couple of straight steps before being asked to repeat the exercise.

▼ INDIRECT BEND

The next stage teaches the horse to move his shoulders, lift his ribcage and be aware of where he is putting his feet. With this exercise, he has reverse or indirect bend – he is looking away from the direction of travel. He has to bring his shoulder and ribcage up and cross his outside front leg over in front of his inside front leg. For indirect bend, the rider's outside hand is slightly higher than the inside hand and the rider's weight is to the inside of the circle and the rider's left (outside) leg is pushing when the horse's inside front leg is on the ground.

COMBINING ALL THREE ELEMENTS

Once your horse is happy doing all these exercises separately, combine them so that you move smoothly from direct bend to indirect bend to moving the hip, back to direct bend and so on. You are now ready for circle work.

HIP DISPLACEMENT

This exercise helps the rider to control his horse's hips in order to produce good canter departs (strike-offs), turns on the forehand and lead changes. It also teaches the rider to use his legs. The horse is bent a little to the inside and the rider's inside leg is used behind the girth to ask him to step over. This request is made in time with the horse's inside hindleg being lifted off the ground. The rider's outside leg is used at the girth to control the horse's ribcage. When you do this exercise, ask your horse to move his hips and take a couple of steps to either right or left: it is like asking him to do a couple of steps of turn on the forehand. Ensure you work on both reins so that he becomes 'ambidextrous'. It's important that the horse steps forward and across with his hindleg.

TIPS

- As you move from one rein to another on direct bend circles make sure you flex your horse to the new inside direction before his shoulder turns.

- As you move from one circle to another, use your inside leg to support your horse's shoulder so that it doesn't fall into the new circle.

- With indirect bend circles, aim to keep your horse relaxed, and keep the bend to the outside by using little squeezes on the rein rather than a constant pressure.

- If your horse can keep a steady walk rhythm during an indirect bend circle then you are doing well.

- With all these exercises use as little as possible to get the desired results.

CIRCLES

To ride a circle well it helps to visualise the line of the circle and imagine that you are sitting above it, with one leg on either side. Your horse's body needs to follow the line of the circle and he needs to stay upright in order to maintain the balance required. Use your outside leg behind the girth to keep his hip up underneath him and your inside leg on the girth to support his shoulder and ribcage. If you feel his quarters swinging out, push them back into line with your outside leg behind the girth; if you feel his outside shoulder drifting out, use your outside leg again but applying the pressure further forward. Learn to ride direct bend circles first, riding on both reins so that you work both sides of your horse's body.

A PUSH-OFF ▶

A push-off is an exercise to help you move out of a circle without allowing your horse to drop his shoulder. You can see the position of the rider's hands, taken to the outside of the circle where he wants the horse to go. On a right rein circle he sits more on his left seatbone, so increasing the weight in his outside stirrup and, therefore, encouraging the horse to move left in order to carry him.

The rider's outside leg is back, to keep the horse's hip underneath his body and the inside leg is at the girth, pushing the horse out to the left. If the rider applies his inside leg aid when he sees the left front leg hit the ground, he knows that the right hindleg is just lifting up and coming forward – and so can be influenced. Remember to start out by trying all these exercises in walk so you have time to co-ordinate your aids.

▼ REIN BACK

As with the other exercises, a Western-trained horse will have learnt to step back in his groundwork preparation before a rider is introduced. When he learns rein back under saddle he is asked for one step at a time and is immediately rewarded for his efforts.

● From halt, keep the weight down in your heels and take a light contact on the reins, rounding your back and sitting slightly to the back of the saddle; combine all this with a verbal request to 'back up'. If your horse steps back release the rein contact, sit in the centre of your saddle again and reward him. Then walk on, halt and repeat the exercise, asking for two steps of rein back.

If he resists, keep a gentle pressure on the reins and reach forward with your leg to tap him lightly on one shoulder. This should encourage him to lift his foot and, as the pressure is on the reins, he should step backwards. If necessary you could face him at the arena fence and repeat the request to help him understand that a backward step is needed.

Advanced skills

The skills outlined below are useful in two ways: firstly, to negotiate hazards you may find while riding out in the countryside or on the trail, and secondly, to enable you to compete in a trail class at a Western show.

◀ NEGOTIATING A BRIDGE

Horses are naturally wary of where they venture: they have survived by being suspicious and testing suspect ground before moving forward. Teaching your horse to walk over strange surfaces, such as this wooden bridge, encourages him to use the logical, problem-solving side of his brain when faced with a challenging situation, rather than reverting to instinctive behaviour and simply running away.

Begin teaching him the basics of this skill in the safety of a round pen or arena. Initially, do the work in-hand; once he is confidently and happily walking over unusual surfaces, start to ride him over them.

Lay a strip of plastic sheeting a couple of feet wide and several feet long in the arena, weighting the ends down with poles so that it doesn't flap about too much and won't come loose. Lead your horse up to the plastic, stop and let him see, sniff, lick or otherwise touch it. Give him time to experiment and work out what the plastic is. Be patient and calm, showing him that there is nothing to fear. If he tries to move away, quietly stop him and bring him back: don't punish him. Curiosity gets the better of all horses and he will make some contact with the plastic – reward every little try with a rub on his head and an encouraging word.

As he becomes more comfortable with the plastic, encourage him to step on it. Step on it yourself, ensuring you are to one side of him so if he suddenly rushes forward you are not in danger. Some horses follow happily, others go backwards or sideways, some leap over. What ever happens just quietly re-direct his attention to the task and reward him when he tries. If he leaps over the plastic, praise him but then take him back around and encourage him to step on it.

Your aim is to have him walking calmly over the plastic, without rushing, without being anxious. When you have achieved this from one direction, turn around and go over it in the opposite direction. He may be a little resistant at first but follow the same plan and he will soon be walking over it from both directions. Once he is confident over plastic, use the same techniques to teach him to walk over wood. Make sure it is strong enough not to break or tip over when he puts his weight on it.

• **Above:** The horse sidepasses (goes sideways without going forwards) up to the gate and stands still while the rider unfastens the latch. The horse then reins back while the rider slides his hand along the gate and opens it so that the pair can pass through, effectively blocking the gate so that any stock in a field cannot escape.

• **Right:** Control of the horse's shoulders and hindquarters is required for the next stages of the manuoeuvre. First he must execute a turn on the haunches and then walk through the gateway.

• **Above:** Then a 45-degree turn on the forehand is needed so that the rider can clear the gate, followed by another turn on the haunches so that the gate can be closed.

• **Right:** As the rider fastens the latch on the gate, the horse stands calmly alongside. Notice how throughout this procedure the horse has been completely relaxed and is able to move equally well in any direction.

◀ GOING THROUGH A GATE

Having a horse that is obedient, soft, supple and responsive can mean the difference between life and death to a working cowboy – for all riders these characteristics come in very useful when negotiating busy roads! This sequence of opening and closing a gate requires the key skills learnt by a Western horse.

▶ A 360-DEGREE TURN

This exercise requires the horse to step into a box and then make a 360-degree turn without stepping forwards or backwards and without touching the poles. The box is only slightly bigger than the length of the horse, so the turn is made using a combination of turn on the forehand and turn on the haunches. The exercise is a good demonstration of how supple and obedient the horse is. In effect he will be rotating around his centre, and the rider has to ask him to take small steps to the side, calmly, to complete the turn.

• The horse is asked to turn on the haunches for a couple of steps so moving the forehand around to the right.

• Next, he is asked for a couple of steps of turn on forehand.

• Followed by turn on haunches.

TIPS

- Your horse won't be able to do these exercises unless he can flex easily at the poll and flex his head and neck sideways without moving his shoulders. To achieve this suppleness takes time and exercises (see pp.144–151).

- If a horse can't do an exercise it may be that your instructions aren't clear or that he is not sufficiently athletic or supple enough for the work demanded. Make sure the basics are in place before trying more advanced manoeuvres. In Western terms of training the basics are equivalent to the first eight rungs on a 10-rung ladder!

- Then a couple of steps of turn on forehand. The sequence is repeated until the 360-degree turn is complete. Great control is needed to alternate between turn on haunches and turn on forehand.

▼ FLYING CHANGE IN LOPE

This is when a horse changes from one leading leg to another while still maintaining the lope. The horse appears to jump in mid-air, changing the sequence of his legs so that instead on being on, for instance, the right lead in lope, he changes to the left lead. This is done without losing any of the rhythm, balance or tempo.

• The horse is on the right lead. The rider is using the left leg and left rein to help elevate the left side of the horse in preparation for the lead change.

• As the horse vaults over the original leading leg both hindlegs come off the ground. The rider asks for the horse's hip to move over by taking his right leg back.

• You can see how the hindlegs come down in a different sequence...

...and how the front leg finishes off the completed stride, with the leading leg having changed. Notice that the rider does not lean over the new inside shoulder. It is a common mistake for riders to lean over in the new direction.

A SPIN

In a spin turn the horse steps around his inside hind pivot leg, keeping one or other front foot on the ground at any given time. Spins are supposed to be executed with rhythm and a certain degree of speed or tempo. The rider asks for a slight bend to the horse's face by laying the outside rein against his neck and indicating a little direction with the inside rein. The rider has his weight in the right seat bone and stays square in the saddle, elevating his inside ribcage. A good spinning horse will stay totally relaxed – the sequence of moves shown in these pictures would occur over a two second timespan.

• The horse's shoulders are level and his left foreleg will cross in front of his right fore to initiate the turn.

• This shows the degree of speed that is needed in the spin – observe the mane flying out.

• The rider is sitting back slightly over the right hindleg (which is the pivot leg). The left hindleg is coming forward to create drive around the turn.

• Coming around to complete the turn. The horse has stayed in his inside pivot leg, the drive coming from the outside hind and two front legs.

Useful Contacts

Association of Chartered Physiotherapists in Animal Therapy
Morland House, Salters Lane, Winchester, Hampshire SO22 5JP

British Horse Society
Stoneleigh Deer Park, Kenilworth, Warwickshire CV8 2XZ

Farriers Registration Council
Sefton House, Adam Court, Newark Road, Peterborough, Lincolnshire PE1 5PP

Society of Master Saddlers
Kettles Farm, Mickfield, Stowmarket, Suffolk IP14 6BY

Lesley Bayley
Equestrian consultant and specialist Lesley Bayley offers freelance instruction in both riding and horse care. She takes a holistic approach to horse and rider, using both traditional and alternative methods, tailored to suit the needs of the individual. Lesley is an Equine Muscle Release Therapy practitioner and is based in Leicestershire. Contact her on 01572 787257
Email:lesley.bayley@virgin.net

Equine Muscle Release Therapy
EMRT is a very gentle, non-invasive therapy, adapted from the Bowen technique that is practised on humans and taught all over the world. The therapy works on the muscle and soft tissue fascia at specific neuro-muscular trigger points of the body. It activates the horse's own healing mechanisms to release muscle spasms, address skeletal imbalances and increase blood supply to the affected areas. It also increases lymphatic drainage so that dysfunction debris, which interferes with healthy muscle and joint activity, is cleared away.

Treatments are carried out with a vet's permission and take approximately 45 minutes. EMRT was developed by Alison Goward in Australia, and the FEI allow the therapy to be used on the day of competition.

For details of accredited EMRT practitioners in the UK contact Sue Connolly on 01789 772413. To contact the Australian office email emrt@ozemail.com.au

ACKNOWLEDGEMENTS

Many thanks to Belstane Marketing Ltd who kindly supplied clothing from the Pikeur range of competition and sports clothing for our riders. Belstane distribute some of the best equestrian brands in the world. For more information visit www.belstane.com.

I would also like to thank the riders who played a key role in the making of this book.

Index

aids 10
  horse's responsiveness to 26
  lateral 103
  leg 20, 104–5, 107, 113, 144
  outside 44
  overuse 15
  rein 105, 144
  seat 73
  weight 90, 101, 144
  Western riding 144
arena 38–45
assessing a horse 26–7
Western riding 142

back
  hollow 66, 83
  muscles 52
  pain 11, 34
  suppleness 63, 67
balance 11, 13, 24, 26, 34
  changing direction 42–5
  half-halt 41
  jumping 123, 134
  lateral work 103
  polework 117
  rider's 10, 36–7
  transitions 70–1, 73, 76
  trot 56
  turns 90
  Western riding 143
bend 94
bends 42–5
  counter 58
  direct bend 145, 147
  indirect bend 145, 146
  loops and serpentines 100
bit 11, 26
  contact 35
body language 11
bounce fences 128–9
Bowen technique 36
box grids 130
box of poles 118
bridges, Western riding 150

canter 60–9
  assessment 61
  collected 63
  counter 63, 101
  departs 147
  extended 62, 84
  giving and retaking reins 68–9

jumping 131, 132
leg yield to 76
lengthened and shortened
  strides 84–9
loops and serpentines 100
medium 62, 84
polework 119
rhythm 61, 66
strike-off 64–5, 117
transitions 61, 64–5, 72–3,
  74, 75–6
Western riding 140, 141, 147
working 62, 84
careless horses 124, 126
centre of gravity 13, 14, 22, 25, 84
circles 50, 90, 92–9, 101
  bend 94
  change of rein 42–5, 74, 96
  half 98–9
  leg yield 107
  polework 119
  transitions 96
  Western riding 147, 148
co-ordination 47, 117, 118, 123,
  134
collection 14, 84, 113
concentration 117
consistency 10
contact 19, 35
cool down 28, 32–3, 131
cornering 24–5, 27, 40
  turning across diagonal 40
  Western riding 143
correction 34
counter bend 58
courses, riding 134–7
  crookedness see straightness

deep frame 28, 32
dental problems 11
diagonals
  changing diagonal 42–5
  trot 56
direct bend 145, 147
direct transitions 74–7
direction, changing 42–5
dog legs 136–7
downward transitions 72–3, 75
dressage tests 34

engagement 22–3, 108
excitable horses 118

fences 124–7
  bounce 128–9
  box grids 130
  crossed poles 124
  riding courses 134–7
  taking at an angle 137
flatwork 47–115
flexibility 35, 100, 121
flying change 154–5
forehand 14
free forward movement 20

gait 20
gates, Western riding 151
giving face 142, 143
grids 123, 124–7, 131
  bounce 128–9
  box 130
ground lines 127
gymnastic exercises 10

hacking 47, 56
half circles 98–9
half-halt 41, 42, 80–1
  downward transitions 73
  loops and serpentines 100–1
  shortening stride 87
  upward transitions 71
halt 74–5, 78–9, 101
hindleg, weak 58
hip displacement 145, 147
hollow outline 66, 83

impulsion 22
impulsive horses 124, 126
indirect bend 145, 146

jaw 26
jog 140
joint flexibility 11, 20, 121
jumping 123–37
  on a circle 132–3
  half-halt 80
  polework 117
  rhythm 132
  rider's jumping position 125
  riding courses 134–7

lameness 55
lateral work 10, 26, 50, 59,
  103–15
leading leg 60

leg aids 20, 104–5, 107, 113,
  144
leg yield 106–7
  to canter 76, 106
lengthened stride 26, 84–5, 88–9
levelness 15, 19
longitudinal work 10
loops 96, 100–1
lope 140, 141
  flying change 154–5
lunge work 15, 34, 59

Mayhew, Bob 139
mental distress 10
Moffett, Heather 73
mouth
  bit contact 35
  sore 11
  wet 35
muscles 11, 15, 47, 84, 123
  overwork 34
  spasm 11
  tension 11

neck muscles 52, 67
neck rein 144
nodding 67

onward-bound 42
outline 26
overbend 49
overwork 11, 34

paces 48–69
  Western riding 140–1
Peace, Michael 53
pelvis, rotation 11
physical discomfort 10–11
pirouettes 87, 112–15
polework 10, 117–21
  crossed poles 124
  ground poles 50
  raised poles 121
  trotting 58
positive reinforcement 10
push-off 148

rein
  aids 105, 144
  changes of 42–5, 74, 96
  contact 52, 81
  giving away 81

giving and retaking 68–9
half-halt 81
holding evenly 19
neck rein 144
uneven contact 35
walk 52
Western riding 144
rein back 82–3, 101, 144
Western riding 149
reining 139
relaxation 11, 12, 20, 26, 34, 47, 118
revision work 28, 30
rewards 10, 142
rhythm 15, 26, 90
canter 61, 66
jumping 132
polework 119, 121
trot 15, 55, 57, 59
walk 15, 48, 50
Western riding 141
rider's balance 10, 36–7
rider's posture 36–7
riding courses 134–7
row of poles 119

seat aid 73
self-carriage 13, 19, 24, 47
semi-circle of poles 120
serpentines 50, 96, 100–1
shoes 11
shortened stride 26, 84–7
shoulder-fore 10, 17, 94, 108–9
shoulder-in 47, 50, 67, 108, 110–11
shoulders 22, 63

sidepass 151
skeletal problems 11
snake trail 145
softening 35
spin 156–7
spine, alignment 16
spiralling in 76, 87, 94, 107
stiffness 34, 48, 55
straightness 16–19, 35, 103
canter 67
halt 78–9
jumping 124
maintaining 42
shoulder-fore 108
shoulder-in 108
walk 48
stride
average length 127
lengthening and shortening 26, 84–9
suppleness 20–1, 22, 47, 63, 70
jumping 123
leg yield 107
loops and serpentines 100–1
shoulder-in 108
turns 90
swinging 53

tack 11
tail 48
tilted head 48
toe, dragging 48
transitions 22, 26, 27, 47, 70–7
canter 61, 64–5, 72–3, 74, 75–6, 147
changes of rein 74

circles 96
direct 74–7
downward 72–3, 75
half-halt 71, 80–1
halt 78–9
lengthened and shortened strides 84–9
loops and serpentines 101
spiralling in 76, 87
trot 58, 70, 72–3, 74–5
upward 70–1, 74
walk 70, 74–5
Western riding 147
within pace 77
trot 29, 54–9
assessment 55
balance 56
collected 57
diagonals 56
extended 57, 84
giving and retaking reins 68–9
lateral work 59
lengthened and shortened strides 84–9
loops and serpentines 100–1
medium 57, 84
polework 119, 121
rhythm 15, 55, 57, 59
transitions 58, 70, 72–3, 74–5, 77
trot to halt transition 74–5
Western riding 140
working 57, 84
turn about the forehand 104

turn on the forehand 104–5
turn on the haunches 112–15
turned loose 145
turns 26, 42–5, 90–1
across diagonal 40
on the forehand 47
half-halt 80
on the haunches 47
spin 156–7
Western riding 152–3, 156–7

upward transitions 70–1, 74

walk 48–53
assessment 48
collected 49
correcting 53
extended 49
free 49, 50, 52
irregular steps 50
loops and serpentines 100–1
medium 49, 50
polework 119
rein contact 52
rhythm 15, 48, 50
swinging 53
transitions 70, 74–5
Western riding 140, 143
warm up 28–9, 100, 131
weight aids 90, 101, 144
Western riding 139–57

A DAVID & CHARLES BOOK

First published in the UK in 2003

Copyright © Lesley Bayley 2003

Distributed in North America
by F&W Publications, Inc.
4700 East Galbraith Road
Cincinnati, OH 45236
1-800-289-0963

ISBN 0 7153 1386 X

Printed in Italy by G. Canale & C. SpA
for David & Charles
Brunel House   Newton Abbot   Devon

Commissioning Editor: Jane Trollope
Art Editor: Sue Cleave
Desk Editor: Shona Wallis
Project Editor: Jo Weeks
Production Controller: Ros Napper

Visit our website at www.davidandcharles.co.uk

David & Charles books are available from all good bookshops; alternatively you can contact our Orderline on (0)1626 334555 or write to us at FREEPOST EX2110, David & Charles Direct, Newton Abbot, TQ12 4ZZ (no stamp required UK mainland).